Graham Uney's Guide

WALKING THE WOLDS

A GUIDE TO DISCOVERING EAST YORKSHIRE ON FOOT

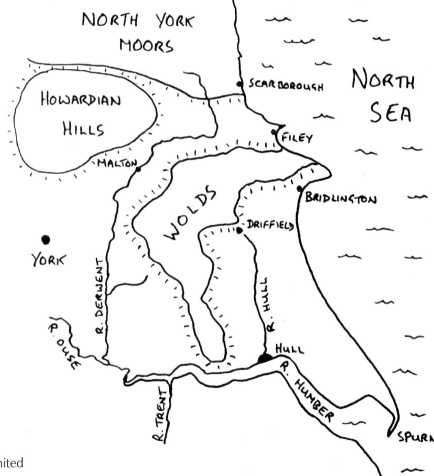

NORTH YORK MOORS

SCARBOROUGH

NORTH SEA

HOWARDIAN HILLS

FILEY

MALTON

WOLDS

BRIDLINGTON

DRIFFIELD

YORK

R. DERWENT

R. HULL

R. OUSE

HULL

R. HUMBER

R. TRENT

SPURN

Highgate of Beverley

Highgate Publications (Beverley) Limited
1999

For Rachel,
with thoughts of many happy times together,
both at home and away.
In anticipation of many more to come.

British Library Cataloguing in Publication Data.
A catalogue record for this book is available from the British Library.

© 1999 Graham Uney

ISBN 1 902645 05 6

Published by

Highgate of Beverley

Highgate Publications (Beverley) Limited
24 Wylies Road, Beverley, HU17 7AP
Telephone (01482) 866826

Produced by

4 Newbegin, Lairgate, Beverley, HU17 8EG
Telephone (01482) 886017

Acknowledgements

As this book has taken shape, I have become more and more indebted to a number of people for their kind help, advice and encouragement, and for this I would like to thank the following: my partner, Rachel, for continuing to support me in my work; my parents, for arranging transportation to and from some of the walks; Monty, for sharing the walks with me and being an ever-enthusiastic companion; and Irene and the boys, for joining Rachel and me on Sunday afternoon strolls through the Yorkshire countryside.

On a more professional note, I must thank John Meehan of the *Hull Daily Mail* for giving me permission to use as a basis for this guide a series of walks that first appeared in the *Hull Daily Mail* during 1998. Chapters 1, 2, 3, 4, 6, 7, 8, 10, 11, and 12 of this book used these articles as a basis upon which to build, and, I hope, improve. I would also like to thank Glen Hood for his correspondence and notes on the Beverley 20; likewise Mr. Dennis Parker for his help with the High Hunsley Circuit and R. Watson with the North Wolds Walk. I am also indebted to the staff of the East Riding of Yorkshire Council Technical Services Department for providing me with advice and contacts, and also to the North Yorkshire County Council Environmental Services for providing details of the Centenary Way. Karen Davies of the Yorkshire Wildlife Trust was a mine of information on their reserves, Chris Toohie, the Countryside Ranger for Millington Wood Nature Reserve, gave kindly of all information relating to that site, and Peter Izzard, the Warden of Tophill Low Nature Reserve, also provided me with enough information, albeit unwittingly, to write Chapter 19. Of course, there may be some whom I have inadvertently omitted, though this is not due to an ungratefulness on my part, more a mental block when it comes to remembering who to thank. Conversely there are numerous local folk, from the Holderness Plain, the Wolds villages and the flatlands of the Derwent carrs who in their own way have contributed to this book, whether by merely passing the time of day, or deliberately providing me with facts and figures: to these unsung heroes I am forever in debt.

Contents

Introduction

In my life as a writer and mountain walking instructor, I am often asked why I have not upped sticks from my home in Hull and moved to a more convenient base from which to explore the mountain regions of Britain. Few who live in and love the East Riding as I do would feel the need to ask such a question. In fact, those who already know the answer, never ask that question, and those who ask the question will never understand the answer.

To be a Yorkshireman is a fine thing, and, while the Dales and Moors of North Yorkshire have an obvious appeal to all who go there, the charms of the East Riding are far more subtle. There is, of course, a definite beauty to the deep, tranquil dales of the Wolds, almost a lost world charm, some might say, but how can you compare the flatlands of Holderness or the Middle Derwent to the majesty of hill-country? These flatlands have a uniqueness and special appeal of their own, and it is hoped that through these walks you will develop a love and understanding for these areas as well as the better- known Wolds.

This book attempts to bring together the very best of the East Riding countryside, though I do admit to stretching the administrative boundaries of our county to include one or two areas that by all accounts truly belong to the East Riding anyway. Surely the Wolds chain is enough of a separate entity as a hill range to avoid being split into two different counties? It would appear not, as parts of the northern Wolds now find themselves included in the already vast county of North Yorkshire. I make no apologies for including walks in this book which fall outside the boundaries of the East Riding, and have determined to draw my own boundaries where I feel they should lie. This conveniently means that within these pages you can find walks throughout the Wolds, plus a handful from the Howardian Hills across the River Derwent. Many would argue that this range does rightly belong to North Yorkshire, which, of course, it does, but I find it sad that these delightful hills are quite often excluded from books on walks in the other areas of North Yorkshire. Guides to the Yorkshire Dales or the North York Moors hardly ever include walks in the Howardian Hills, mainly because they are also excluded from both of those National Parks. And so I have taken the decision to include them here. This is not to say that the East Riding does not have enough of interest to stand alone. I have included these walks simply because I'm sure you will delight in exploring them along with the East Riding.

Within each chapter I have included details of how to find the start of the walk, as well as notes on the distance covered and how long you should allow to complete the walk. I have also tried to introduce you to the often fascinating history and wildlife that goes with each area in the hope that this will heighten your enjoyment both while out on the walk and also while at home prior to, and after, each trip. Sketch maps accompany all chapters, although it is recommended that you use the relevant Ordnance Survey maps whilst out on the walks. The following will be found to be essential – Landranger Series (pink maps) Numbers 100, 101, 106 and 107.

Chapter One

Walking around Huggate Wold

This is a pleasant circular walk of about nine miles, and is the ideal introduction to the delightful chalky dales around the village of Huggate. Huggate lies a couple of miles south of one of the highest parts of the A166 York to Driffield road, and about three miles north of Warter, which is on the B1246 Pocklington to Driffield road.

The focal point of village life in Huggate is the popular Wolds Inn, a good place to start and finish this walk. A few hundred metres west of the inn, a minor road turns right and gradually drops downhill through the village, passing by the 339-foot-deep well in the centre of the village green. A Mr. James Lollit sunk this well through the soft strata of porous Wolds chalk to reach the permanent water-table in the 1760s, an accomplishment which earned him a grand payment of 27 guineas. Today the well is sealed, the village taking its water from a treatment works a couple of hundred metres further down the lane. A sign has been erected by the well telling of its claim to be the deepest in England.

The road splits into two, passing around either side of the green with its clutch of cottages, and you can follow either to the medieval church of St. Mary's. The lane to the right also passes the village duck pond, man-made as many originally were in the Wolds, by importing boulder clay from the flatlands of the Holderness Plain to the east, and lining the dug-out pit to hold the water. Mallards and the occasional coot or moorhen frequent its shady waters today.

If time is not in short supply, it is worth exploring the

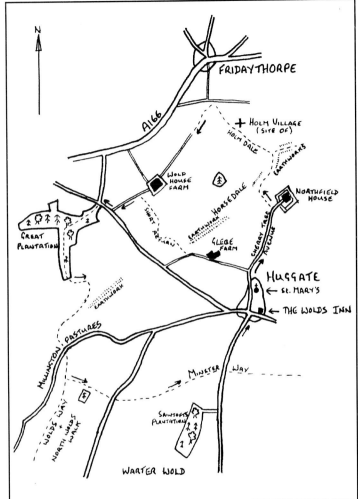

church itself before getting underway with the walk. Most of the present architecture of St. Mary's belongs to the time of the Normans, including the chancel arch and two windows which have been moved from elsewhere. Underneath the 15th-century clerestory there are good examples of arcades from the end of the 12th century.

Perhaps the most remarkable thing about the church, however, is a small plaque on a wall beneath the tower. It reads: 'This spire was repaired in 1830 by T. Filey without scaffolding. T. Cross. J. Turner. Churchwardens.' A truly remarkable feat of steeple-jacking.

After visiting St. Mary's, continue on the northward-bound lane, passing the water treatment works on the right. A farm track joins ours from Glebe Farm to the left, signposted as the Wolds Way, and the lane continues, still tarmac covered, passing a stile leading to the grassy Cow Dale on the right. The lane is a delight, especially in spring when the avenue of young cherry trees (ornamental *Prunus* cultivars) that line either side are in full flower, blossoming pale pink and off-white in the warming sun. Our path turns left off the metalled lane, which is the driveway to the large farmhouse and attendant buildings of Northfield Farm. About 300 yards before the farm, a public bridleway sign points to the north-west and follows the Wolds Way alongside a hawthorn hedge and through a gate to descend into Horse Dale. The path slants diagonally rightwards down into the grassy valley bottom to a junction of fences. On the descending path, a series of contouring earthworks are crossed, looking not unlike grassy sheep trods. From the bottom, a gate and stile on the left lead into the long, deep trough of Holm Dale beside a small stand of deciduous trees, while straight ahead, down the valley, the way curves out of sight into Harper Dale.

The wonderful Holm Dale, like many others

St. Mary's Church at Huggate.

in the chalky Wolds, is a favourite haunt of orange tip and common blue butterflies. The former is usually only widespread in the south of England, and the common blue is becoming anything but common. This delightfully tiny species flies on a wingspan of only 2.5 cm, and in its caterpillar stage depends on the yellow flowered legumes of the trefoil family for its chief food source. The bird's foot trefoil flourishes in many parts of the Yorkshire Wolds, and like all legumes, can be recognised by its pea-like flowers.

Another insect that depends on the trefoils for food is the locally common six-spot burnet. This fearsome looking moth has dark metallic blue fore-wings, appearing almost black, distinguished by six vermilion dots on each wing. It is a day-flying moth, and so can often be seen during the months of summer.

High up to the east, above Holm Dale, is the site of Holm village, originally settled, like many other Wolds villages, by the invading La Tène people of France during the late Iron Age, perhaps 2,200 years ago, and certainly before the Roman invasion of Britain in AD43. Earthworks and dikes can still be seen in many of the dry valleys and on surrounding hillsides around this area, almost definitely dug as primitive boundary markers. This village was completely wiped out by the bubonic plague, or Black Death, and there is little trace of it today.

The path continues following the Wolds Way and leads gently uphill throughout the length of Holm Dale to

The path down to where Horse Dale, Holm Dale and Harper Dale converge.

where a gate and stile lead out to a crossroads of muddy lanes. Cowpasture Road heads off to the west, while Huggate Lane leads into Fridaythorpe with the Manor House and Cross Keys pubs straight ahead. Eastwards lies Green Lane, the old boundary between the open field systems of Fridaythorpe and Holm villages. These are all public by-ways now.

However, our way doesn't lie through the gate at all. From the huge ash and chestnut trees which stand guard over the stile, turn to the south-west and follow the field boundary on its southern side. The way is obvious, being well marked and following, as it does, a good farm track throughout. This track passes through some of the chalkiest fields I have ever seen, seemingly composed more of chalk than good arable soil, although, if the healthy looking crops which flourish in these fields are anything to go by, this calciferous loam doesn't seem to have a detrimental effect on the harvest.

Before long, the outbuildings of a large farm complex are reached, and you should find yourself crossing the huge farm yard at Huggate Wold House. Aim for a gap between the large metal barn and a new gate where a footpath sign points across a second, more traditional, arched-barn enclosed yard. Follow the drive out to York Lane, the minor road between Huggate and the A166.

On York Lane, turn right for 300 yards, then turn left down a muddy track into Great Plantation. Although this is owned by the Forestry Commission (or Forestry Enterprise as they like to be called these days), there is a public bridleway underfoot, and they have no objection to people walking along the track in the valley bottom, known as Greenwick Dale. Indeed it is often very popular at weekends. Continue through the mixed woodland of larch, beech and sycamore to a gate leading into Tun Dale, making sure, of course, that you close and latch it behind you – a couple of hundred hungry sheep could cause havoc in a delicate woodland.

The path leads out of Great Plantation and on through a flower-filled meadow. This is typical Wolds scenery with an abundance of wild plants indigenous to chalky soil; cowslips, bee orchid, forget-me-nots, pink campion, field poppies and scabious can often be found, but please leave them for others to enjoy. After a double gate in Frendel Dale the minor road to Millington is reached. Crossing almost straight over this, a path climbs uphill on the left side of a gappy hawthorn hedge and on, to skirt around the western side of Jessop's Plantation. These few miles follow the course of the North Wolds Walk, an excellent 20-mile-long challenge hike, described in full later in this book. However, today we only follow it for a short stretch, over this hill and down into yet another grassy dale known locally as Nettle Dale. Golden spikes of gorse, another member of the legume order of plants, cloak the hillside, proving what a diverse selection of plants that order includes. A path leads up the opposite hillside, and, about halfway up, a line of mature hawthorns contours the pasture. A Minster Way sign points eastwards above these miniature trees. Aim for the wood up on the skyline where a line of telegraph poles gains the ridge from the dale bottom. The path, which is still signposted 'Minster Way', goes through a gate here, and then borders field boundaries before crossing Cobdale Lane at Cobdale Cottage.

The track now runs along the Hawold Bridle Road, a good grassy lane which contours high above the deep valleys around Warter Wold to the south. Woods again predominate in these dales, and abound with wonderful sounding names such as 'Saintofts Plantation' and 'Golden Valley Plantation'. Continuing eastwards on Hawold Bridle Road, you come to yet another minor road, known as Mill Lane, which heads north, passing by three concrete areas which were constructed for tank training during the 1939-1945 war. Mill Lane leads back to the centre of Huggate within a mile, rising steadily before descending into the fold of the hills where the village nestles.

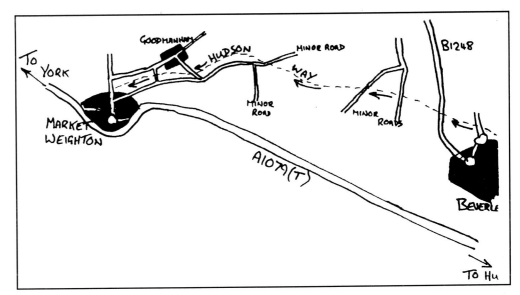

Chapter Two

Walking the Hudson Way

It's hard to imagine a time before the railway was ever constructed through the quiet countryside of tranquil dales and rolling chalk hills which hold in their sheltered corners the sleepy villages of Cherry Burton, Etton and Goodmanham. Certainly, as you walk along the disused line today, you couldn't possibly feel that the cinder track underfoot, and the odd abandoned railway buildings alongside, are anything but part of the landscape. Unnatural, yes, but they blend into the surroundings so well that they do in fact add to the overall essence and charming beauty of the Wolds scenery.

The railway was opened in 1865 as a link with the line which came down from Driffield. This was all part of a proposal to connect the Hull-Barnsley line to Scarborough, carrying people from the industrial heartlands of the West Riding to the east coast during summer. Like so many other rural branch lines throughout the country, this line through the Wolds became a victim of 'Beeching's Axe' in November 1965, and was closed down.

Although only eleven miles long, being along an old railway line this is a linear walk, leaving the walker with the problem of organising transport from the finish back to the start. A car park and picnic site just north of Beverley and half a mile east of a roundabout on the A164 to Driffield is the official start. A junction, 50 yards west of the new Hayfield Inn, leads into this car park.

There is little chance of losing your way on this walk: it is simply a matter of gaining the raised embankment of the railway and heading west. The pleasant little town of Market Weighton is your final destination, but you should allow a good four hours of fairly gentle walking, mainly on the flat with just the odd, barely perceptible gradient, to get there.

In only a short distance, about three quarters of a mile from the start, this, the Hudson Way, named after George Hudson, whose concept it was to have his own railway network in the East Riding, passes via a brick bridge beneath the traffic whizzing north on the A164 to Driffield.

During the next mile or so, the scenery is typical of this part of the Wolds. Being east of the main Wolds chain of chalky low hills, the view backwards extends over the vast arable fields of this, the edge of the flatlands which is the Holderness Plain.

After passing below another brick bridge, the greens and fairways of the relatively new Cherry Burton Golf Course run parallel to the track on the left.

Within another three quarters of a mile, the walker on the Hudson Way comes across what is the only real hazard along the entire eleven miles, the B1248. This busy road links Beverley via the roundabout at Molescroft to Wetwang and ultimately Malton, Pickering and the North York Moors National Park. The hazard comes from crossing the road. Steps lead down to the roadside beneath a canopy of trees, and (after a quick dash), others climb up a steep bank on the opposite side of the road.

The track becomes quite muddy for a while. Even in the driest of summer weather, it takes a good few days to dry out thoroughly. Without even realising it, the walker is now entering the eastern slope of the Yorkshire Wolds proper.

Soon after passing beneath the next bridge, which takes the minor road from Cherry Burton to Etton, an old mill, minus its sails, is passed on the right beside the well maintained small-holding at Mill Farm. From here onwards, the scenery improves and the already abundant wildlife increases. Rabbits have abounded all along this track, but here are joined by the odd hare or perhaps even a fox, weasel or stoat.

The humble rabbit must surely be the most familiar of our wild mammals. What is not often appreciated is that it is not truly a British species. Originally it came from the Iberian Peninsular and areas of southern France, but has spread throughout western Europe both naturally and by introduction to Britain by the Normans, although some authorities suspect that the Romans may have attempted an unsuccessful introduction of the

Kiplingcotes Station on the Hudson Way.

species a thousand years prior to that. Myxomatosis helped to cull the heavy populations in 1954 and 1955, though since then the numbers have pretty much stabilised, seeming to build up over several years, then suffering an alarming crash. Rabbits pose a very serious threat to British agricultural practices, often devastating crops at an alarming rate. The rabbit is easily distinguishable from the much bigger brown hare, as that species has very long ears, prominently black tipped, and over-sized hind legs. The hare is also considered an agricultural pest, but is protected by game laws. The population of the brown hare has dropped drastically in the Wolds over the last few decades, but the reasons for this are not clear.

Bird-life thrives in the hawthorn and elderberry bushes which line the track, with green and gold finches, blue and great tits, warblers, yellowhammers and that agile, hovering raptor, the kestrel, living alongside the more familiar house sparrows, blackbirds, robins and thrushes. Pheasants and partridges are also a common sight on the farmland and in the woods of the area.

Crossing another minor road, the track bends round to the right in a long curve, crosses a farm track at Michael's Bridge, no longer there, then again bends back to the left near Maiden's Grave on Etton Wold. A long straight section leads to the old station at Kiplingcotes. The station building itself is now a house, and the owner sells ice creams and other refreshments to the passing

Sunset over South Dalton.

walker. There is a car park here which is popular with people wishing to walk just a short section of the way.

Just a mile or so to the north of the station lies the route of England's oldest horse race, the celebrated Kiplingcotes Derby. It is known that the race first started in 1519, when a group of 'hunting gentlemen' drew up a list of rules, although the earliest recorded evidence of the Derby actually taking place dates back to 1555. The gruelling four-and-a-half-mile-long course was a regular fixture in the *Racing Calendar* until 1789, when a revision of the established racing laws meant that a minimum stake of £100 had to be in place for a race to be included in the calendar. The race is still run annually today, held on the third Thursday in March, regardless of the weather. Any horse can enter, not only thoroughbreds, and, although a bookmaker was always present in the past, this practice is not always carried out. Spectators are welcome, and local TV coverage ensures its popularity.

From Kiplingcotes Station the track takes to the lush valley of Goodmanham Dale. Scenically, this is my favourite section of the entire walk. At the Kiplingcotes Chalk Pit, you can leave the track for a while to explore this peaceful nature reserve. It is maintained by the Yorkshire Wildlife Trust which allows public access to most areas, but quite rightly insists that no dogs be taken onto the reserve. Other access details are on a notice board at the entrance and should be adhered to. A Nature Trail takes you around the grassy meadows and along the top of a chalk scree slope where benches are provided for admiring the views across the dale. In all, the reserve covers around nine and a half acres of land, and provides an excellent example of a typical Wolds landscape and wildflower habitat. Originally the site was quarried to supply chalk for the embankments during the building of the railway, though quarrying here continued until 1902. In 1965 the Yorkshire Wildlife Trust leased the site from the British Railways Board and was eventually able to purchase the reserve in 1974. Today it is managed under a number of different techniques forming patchworks of varying successions of plant growth. It is this collection of different habitats that attracts such a wide variety of flora and fauna species. For example, the reserve has records of over 200 flowering plant species, 250 invertebrate and 80 bird species. Small mammals are also well represented.

The Hudson Way is now coming to an end. After crossing yet another minor road, near the source of the tiny, fast-flowing Mill Beck, it runs beside the waters of this stream down Spring Dale, passing close by the hidden St. Helen's Well before dipping beneath the last bridge before entering Market Weighton. Near to the source of Mill Beck there is another Yorkshire Wildlife Trust property, Rifle Butts Quarry. The chief source of interest here is geological, in that the walls of the quarry are composed of unusually layered red and white chalk. This reserve, however, is not open to the public.

Market Weighton is an old market town centred on a turnpike. The most famous son of the town is William Bradley, the renowned giant of the fairgrounds and freak-shows. At 7 ft. 9 in high and weighing in at 27 stones, he is wrongly attributed in the record books as being England's tallest man, an honour that rightly belongs to another Yorkshireman, Henry Cooper, often called 'The Scugdale Giant'. Henry was born in the village of Swainby on the North York Moors, and towered over William Bradley by a staggering 9 inches! He toured America with Barnum in the 1880s but was never officially measured for the record books. Both men passed away at a very early age, Bradley dying in 1820 at only 33, and Cooper in the early years of this century at 32. This abnormality is without doubt linked with that of their incredible size. William Bradley's grave can be visited in the graveyard of All Saints parish church in Market Weighton. Once you have finished looking round the town, a regular bus service connects Market Weighton with Beverley, and back to the start of this walk.

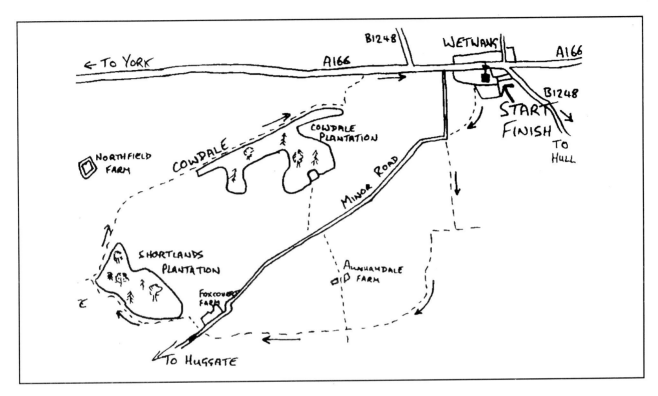

Chapter Three

Walking around Wetwang

Wetwang lies about six miles west of Driffield on the busy A166, which links that pleasant market town with York. The Black Swan Inn is the focal point of the village, being adjacent to the village duck pond with its attendant black swans, and gives as good a place as any to start and finish this walk. The pond itself is man-made, being lined with boulder clay, though it used to be said that the very name of the village itself derives from the Old Norse for 'wet place', surely an oddity in the dry valleys of our eastern chalk hills. There is, however, some

evidence to prove that the true derivation of 'Wetwang' is the Icelandic term *'vaet-vangr'* – meaning a field of summons for a trial. Graves and entrenchments have been found around the village that date back to the Ancient Britons of the Viking invasions, so there is probably some truth in this theory of the origin of the strange name of Wetwang. The pond is known to have been there for over 600 years, and there is another, smaller pond at the western end of the village that is almost as old.

The lane beside the church of St. Nicholas, with its lychgate of oak and stone and remains of an ancient cross, and which in part dates back to the 12th century, leads south around a bend to a small village school on the corner of another minor lane. Follow this into Southfield Road to a place where a public footpath sign points diagonally across a field.

Follow the well-worn path downhill across the middle of the field to a corner where a hawthorn hedge begins, and runs parallel to the path heading west towards a minor road known as Thorndale Lane. At the lane, which takes infrequent traffic to Huggate, turn left for a short distance until it takes a sharp right, then follow a public bridleway straight ahead into the small valley of Thorn Dale itself. Continuing along this bridleway, a T-junction is reached at a point where a long narrow wood of elder and ash runs west to east with a trod known as Green Lane passing along it. Take the lane, which is not much more than a path through the narrow copse, to the right from the junction.

This slender corridor of wildlife is one of the best places that I know of in the Wolds to gather the strange-looking fungus known as the Jew's ear. It grows in clusters along the branches of deciduous trees and shrubs, but seems to favour elder. It closely resembles a reddish brown ear, vaguely translucent with wrinkles, looking for all the world like veins. It can be found year round, though it is usually only seen in the winter months when the leaves have fallen from the trees. Many people are familiar with the bizarre brackets, but few realise that they are actually edible when gathered young. They can be used in stews and even fried, but they do have a tendency to explode out of the pan if you try the latter. It is wise to cook them well, as they are leathery and indigestible when under-cooked, but, unless you are absolutely certain of positively identifying them, you shouldn't attempt to gather them at all. A glance at a specialist book on fungi should suffice to learn what to look for, for there are no poisonous species that even vaguely resemble the juicy Jew's ear.

Heading west along the Green Lane through the wood, as chaffinches flit from branch to branch, the path soon emerges onto the open fields of Tibthorpe Wold, and takes to the perimeter of these huge arable acres in a large irregular curve, heading first south, then south-west, and finally round to the west near the open ridge known as Christcross Close. Throughout its length, the path is easy to follow, and, after a mile and a half, it crosses a chalky farm track above Aunham Dale, before continuing west towards Foxcovert Farm on the minor road from Wetwang to Huggate. All along this track a hawthorn hedge runs alongside and is occasionally interspersed with other trees and shrubs including ash, elderberry, dog rose and field maple. I have even seen a variegated bush of the elderberry growing in here, though this is usually only a cultivated garden species. On this oddity each individual leaf is edged with a slim stripe of custard yellow, set off well against the vivid green of the leaf's interior.

Hares are a common sight in this area. At one point, just beyond the farm track at Christcross Close, I once saw five brown hares basking in the faint sun of an early April. They remained there, totally unaware of my presence as I stood stock-still in the open, up-wind of them, until one happened to stretch and glanced in my direction. Within thirty seconds, all five had gone, running in seemingly awkward jumps on over-sized hind legs across the newly tilled soil of the fields to the north. At any other time of year this would have been extremely unusual, as the brown hare is very much a solitary creature. Only during the breeding season do they come together, when the males fight or 'box' for the mating rights of a female. It is this spectacle that has given rise to the saying 'Mad as a March Hare'. They are usually described as a nocturnal animal, but there is always a strong chance of catching a glimpse of one during the day. Although their food source is usually nothing more than grass, they do on occasion devastate root crops, cereals and also eat the bark off young trees. It is this that has led them to become hated by the farmer. They make their home in a shallow depression on the ground, known as a form, unlike the warren-digging habits of the smaller rabbit, and can have two to four young (leverets) each year.

The public footpath bends round to the right as it nears a small plantation before crossing the minor road at Foxcovert Farm. This small collection of farm buildings is almost surrounded by trees and always seems to be a pleasant, peaceful place. A farm track separates a couple of small fields which often play home to a number of sheep and chickens. This track is just west of the farm itself, and, as it passes through the wood which surrounds the farm, it turns left alongside a small thicket of confers to go through a series of gates and into Shortlands Dale. Be very careful of the fence which borders the path on the right as it descends to the bottom of the dale. It is usually electrified to keep the rams in one half of the field separated from the ewes and lambs in the other. Although of only a low voltage, the current is still sufficient to give you an unpleasant shock. I came this way during lambing time one year, and was surprised to see countless young lambs walk into this fence to receive a nasty shock. They each jumped away in fright, and then walked into it again just a few yards further on. No doubt they do eventually get the message!

As the path descends, rabbits and pheasants usually scatter to all sides. The path here runs along the grassy valley bottom with a steep hillside covered with the mixed woodland of Shortlands Plantation rising to the right. Within half a mile, another valley, known as Oxlands Dale comes in from the left.

In a short while, after passing through a couple of gates (remembering to close them again after you), you reach a stile which crosses another fence to join the White

The author near the head of Cowdale.

Hill Path coming downhill from the direction of Huggate to the left. This stile lies beside a wonderful old ash tree.

Over the years the keys of this proud specimen must have carried thousands of seeds on the wind, far into Shortlands Plantation and Rabbit Wood, germinating there among the rich humus of the forest floor, and so continuing the line of the noble *Fraxinus* family. The huge girth of the tree gives us some idea of its age, though, of course, we would have to chop it down to count the growth rings to know its exact age, and no lover of the countryside would wish for that to happen. In winter, when the trees are bare, the ash is perhaps one of the easiest to recognise. Each twig on the tree is lined with pairs of black buds bursting through the silvery bark, and is tipped by a single, larger black bud. Ash trees are common in the Wolds due to the fact that they thrive on the lime-rich soils of the chalk beds. They have a relatively short growing season each summer, as they leaf out later than most other trees of Britain, and lose them again very early in the autumn. The timing of the leaf burst is the subject of a widespread country rhyme which is said to predict the weather for the coming season:

> Oak before ash . . . we're in for a splash;
> Ash before oak . . . we're in for a soak!

Another strange thing about the ash tree is that its flowers are often either all male, or all female, and it can change its sex from year to year, or even choose to be bisexual for a year!

From the large ash by the stile, the path sweeps down the main valley of Cowdale, initially called Rabbit Dale, around to the right. The path follows the valley bottom throughout, but later, after climbing over a couple of stiles, runs alongside the woods of Cowdale Plantation.

After just over two miles, the woods on the right end and the track takes a bend to the right and then a sharp turn left below Cinquefoil Hill. A signpost points the way up a steep grassy bank before ending at a broken stile on the edge of West Field. The path here actually cuts diagonally across the corner of the field, before crossing a much wider field to gain the main A166 less than a mile west of Wetwang. This road is very busy, but the grass verge is wide enough to walk on, safely back to the start, after around eight miles of good walking.

Chapter Four

Discovering the deserted medieval village of Wharram Percy

The Wharram-le-Street of today lies along the busy B1248, from Wetwang to Malton, but it is known that this tiny village has been a settlement since Roman times. Indeed, it actually lies on the course of a Roman road, hence the name. After the Romans, came the Anglo-Saxons of Germanic origin, and their influence can still be seen in the village in the form of a Saxon tower on the church. Just one mile north-east of Wharram-le-Street is the village of Duggleby, with nearby Duggleby Howe in a field beside the road. This is the largest known Neolithic barrow (grave-mound or tumulus) in Britain, pre-dating the Romans by perhaps two thousand years.

Just south of Wharram-le-Street, a minor road turns left off the B1248, and is signposted 'Wharram Percy – Medieval Monument'. Within a hundred yards, this minor lane bends around to the left and continues past Bella Farm to a car park near a small stand of conifer trees. This is the start of our walk.

Leaving the car here, resist the temptation to follow the signs directly downhill to the medieval village of Wharram Percy. Our route will come up along that path within just two or three miles of easy walking and we will take in a tour of the deserted village itself later on. From the car park, take the minor road back past Bella Farm to the bend just before it joins the B1248. A public footpath, signposted 'Wolds Way' and 'Centenary Way', goes straight ahead on the left-hand side of a hedge.

The Centenary Way is a little-known 84-mile-long-distance footpath from Filey Brigg to York Minster. It was devised by North Yorkshire County Council to celebrate 100 years of County Councils. The Way was officially opened on 8 December 1989 by the former Olympic

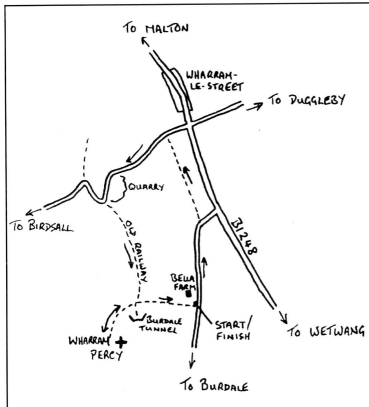

TO MALTON

WHARRAM-
LE-STREET

TO DUGGLEBY

TO BIRDSALL

QUARRY

OLD RAILWAY

B1248

BELLA
FARM

BURDALE
TUNNEL

START/
FINISH

TO WETWANG

WHARRAM
PERCY

TO BURDALE

guelder rose, but, whereas that prefers dank woodlands, the wayfaring tree thrives on open sunny sites. As it is really only a wild species in the south of England, it is likely that those in this hedge have been planted by man. It has large, flat-topped heads of tiny white flowers from April to June, which in turn produce red berries, turning black as they ripen.

This is one of the most panoramic sections of the walk, and indeed is among the best viewing points in the whole of the Wolds. Across the wide glacial valley of the Vale of Pickering, once swamped by a huge ice encased lake system, the dark smudge of the North York Moors National Park rises beyond the red pantiled roofs of Malton and Norton on the River Derwent, mightiest of the East Riding rivers. This northern scarp of the Wolds, around these parts known as the Birdsall Brow, but continuing in a vague line to the north-east along East Heslerton Brow, Sherburn Brow and Staxton Brow, all the way to the coast between Filey Brigg and Flamborough Head, is the furthest northern extent of chalk hills in the whole of the British Isles.

Within 300 yards, the path gains another minor road beside some cottages. Climb over the stile here and follow the road to the left down into a valley.

Just before you reach the valley bottom, a gateway on the left gives access to Wharram Quarry, now a nature reserve maintained by the Yorkshire Wildlife Trust. Being the habitat of a host of rare plants endemic to chalky districts, access is granted only to members of the Trust. Although you may be tempted to have a look, please respect this rule and keep out. Details of how to become a member of the Yorkshire Wildlife Trust are given in an appendix to this book.

Beyond the quarry, along the lane, a group of cottages

athlete and mountaineer, Chris Brasher, though since then there have been one or two access problems along the way and North Yorkshire County Council are undertaking a thorough survey of the route to remedy this.

While you walk along this short section of the path, take a look at the large number of different species of trees and shrubs that make up the hedge on the right. Although predominantly hawthorn, you will be able to see dog-rose, beech, elderberry, ash, crab-apple and the *viburnum* known as the wayfaring tree. This is very similar to the other, more common *viburnum* species, the is clustered around the old Wharram Station buildings. The railway was opened in 1853 as a means of transporting the thousands of tonnes of chalk that was being quarried in the area to the main railway networks of the country, and also to provide the local farmers with a valuable link to the market towns of Malton and Driffield, which stood at either end of the line. It is now disused, having taken its last cargo of freight in 1958, but at least today it provides the walker with an excellent public footpath leading to Wharram Percy.

Leave the metalled road and go left between the cottages, following the cinder track of the old railway beside a rushing stream. For part of the way, the stream flows along a narrow 'canal', about two feet across and just a few inches deep, full of bright green duckweed in the slow-moving margins and sumps formed where the canal sides have collapsed. Trees have closed in to form a canopy overhead, and many animals and birds frequent the woods of this area. It is quite possible that you may be able to spot chaffinches, blue and great tits, goldfinches, the odd shy wren and perhaps even make out the tracks of a fox along the muddy edges of the track. Blackbirds, robins, thrushes, dunnocks and fieldfares are also usually present, although fieldfares only flock in large numbers during the winter months, being a scarce breeder in this country.

If you catch sight of the little jenny wren in the vegetation, you should consider yourself quite lucky,

Wharram Percy.

14

for it is one of the smallest British birds, being little more than three inches long. Its main characteristics are its short tail, always set at a jaunty angle to its body, and its loud ripping warble for a song, interspersed with occasional hearty '*tic-tics*'. It can be hard to spot, as it flits from perch to perch, but doesn't actually appear to be timid. It is believed that there are around ten million pairs of these charming little birds in Britain today.

Within a mile of gaining the railway track, you come to a path which descends the hill towards you on the left, crosses our track and, passing through a kissing-gate, climbs diagonally leftwards across the open hillside to the right. Alongside this kissing-gate is a plaque describing what can be seen of the medieval village of Wharram Percy. This site is owned by English Heritage who allow free access to the public.

The continuation of the railway line delves almost immediately into the bowels of the earth beyond the junction of paths. This is the Burdale railway tunnel. Over a period of six years the railway engineers worked on this mile-long tunnel, but today it is blocked off to deter those who may wish to explore its hidden secrets.

Go through the kissing-gate on the right and keep to the track. The first buildings to come into view are the top of the steeple of St. Martin's Church and an old farmhouse built in the mid-19th century. As you approach, it soon becomes obvious that this farmhouse stands on the site of a much older collection of buildings. Archaeologists first began researching this site in the 1950s and 60s after discovering tell-tale signs of ancient settlements from aerial photographs. Leading authorities from all over the world have flocked to Wharram Percy ever since to study how the ancient Britons lived. A book is available, published by English Heritage, which describes the site in detail and the many phases of archaeological digs which uncovered the remains that we see today.

The church itself has seen many changes over the years and is believed to date back as far as the 10th century when it was probably no more than of timber and cob construction [cob being a walling material, made of compressed earth, clay or chalk, usually reinforced with straw]. Plaques dotted around the church, and indeed the whole site, explain the history of Wharram Percy in greater detail. The church today is without a roof, but the steeple remains intact. The gravestones in the churchyard are also interesting to read, although some are almost illegible due to weathering over the centuries.

Beyond the church to the south is a man-made pond which has served as an ancient sheep-dip, a mill-pool and a fish pond. You can walk across the dam of clay and around the perimeter of the pond, although this path is sometimes boggy.

Other kissing-gates give access to the hillside above the church where remains of medieval longhouses can be seen. Signs explain that other houses dating to even earlier times have been found on the same site and give details of where and what to look for.

When you have finished looking around Wharram Percy, perhaps staying a while for a picnic, remembering, of course, to take home all your rubbish, return along the path to the kissing-gate and cross straight over the railway track to gain the path straight ahead. This climbs steeply up through a nice open pasture of wild flowers and alongside a hedge back to the car park.

Chapter Five

The Beverley 20

This long-distance, challenging walk was the brain-child of Mr. Glen Hood, a teacher at the now demolished Shakespeare Junior High School in Hull. During his time there, many of his pupils showed a good deal of interest in the now famous Lyke Wake Walk, which runs across the North York Moors National Park from Osmotherley to Ravenscar, but Mr. Hood thought that this would be a bit too much of a challenge for his inexperienced walking charges. He suggested that they first take on a local walk, both as a taster for what would be expected of them should they go on to attempt the Lyke Wake Walk, and also as a training exercise.

He pored over maps looking for a suitable route, having, as he did, an idea for a walk of around 20 miles in length. At last, he, fellow teachers and a party of pupils set off to walk the first-ever Beverley 20.

That original route followed the banks of the Humber westwards to Welton Waters from a start to the east of the Humber Bridge before heading north, inland towards Skidby, Walkington, and ultimately Beverley. With increasing building activity around some parts of the route, most notably to the south of Beverley, and the unpopularity of a few sections of the route, minor alterations were made to leave us with the route we have today – possibly the very finest challenging walk in the southern half of the Yorkshire Wolds.

The walk starts at the Humber Bridge car park to the west of Hessle. At the southern end of the car park a kissing-gate leads to the top of a flight of steps and down into the woods of the Humber Bridge Country Park. In summer the trees in these woods are alive with those wonderfully vocal birds, the various members of the warbler family.

Soon after you enter the wood, two short tunnels lead

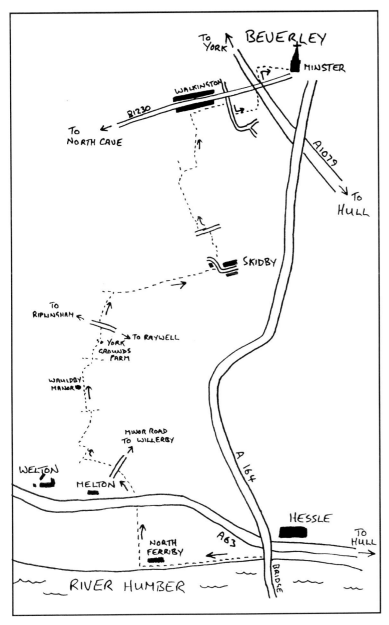

out to the foreshore and the chalky banks of the Humber Estuary. Near the large pub on the foreshore take to the beach and head west. It is usual for walkers to stay on the beach, although a bit of a path can be found along the other side of a rough hedge.

In winter the mud-flats around this area form an important habitat for a number of wader species. These inevitably long-legged birds feed by probing the mud for tiny molluscs and crustaceans. Redshank are the most obvious, strutting around on bright red legs and probing for food with an equally bright red bill. Other waders that can be seen here include dunlin, red knot, turnstone, grey and golden plovers along with the occasional bar-tailed godwit.

Within three miles the way passes a car park at North Ferriby, a popular spot with dog walkers, bird watchers and families skimming stones. Continuing alongside Redcliff Sands, you come to some wooden steps on the right which soon lead into the broad-leaved wood of Long Plantation. This runs northwards and forms the western boundary of the village. A good path, sometimes muddy, is followed through the wood, crossing a railway line via a bridge before emerging from the trees onto the very busy A63 dual-carriageway. The path continues into the wood across this road, but great care is needed in crossing, and, if in doubt, you should use the footbridge which lies a little way to the left.

Once across, the path runs gently uphill in Terrace Plantation. The way is still obvious as this part of the Beverley 20 shares the route of the only official long-distance footpath in the East Riding – the Wolds Way.

At the top of Melton Hill, the path begins its gradual descent, passing the Scout huts at Melton Bottoms before reaching the minor road into the village of Melton. Our way lies straight ahead again, after carefully crossing the road. A good track climbs uphill, alongside the devastating sight of the Melton Bottoms Chalk Quarry to the north. This track can be followed throughout, although the actual route turns sharp left into Bow Plantation before running parallel to the main track.

Within half a mile, the track descends slightly, and, at a place where the public footpath emerges from Bow Plantation, a rough lane climbs out of Welton Dale from the left and continues at right angles to our track to the right. Follow this track, still skirting the quarry. Luckily,

this is out of sight behind a screen of larch fencing and clumped saplings. The way takes a sharp left, then a sharp right after 200 yards, contouring along the upper slopes of the delightful Welton Dale, a route taken in the next chapter of this book. Our path soon leaves the quarry behind to the right, but continues beside the mixed scrub and trees of Welton Wold Plantation on the left.

After about a mile, the path joins a private concrete drive which crosses at right angles. Cross straight over and follow footpath signs around a hedge and through a narrow belt of trees before heading north for Wauldby Manor Farm. Here a duck pond is reached just before the main farm buildings, which should be kept on the left as you continue north along a good track. This curves around a low hump known as Turtle Hill before crossing a junction of public footpaths. Here we leave the Wolds Way as it continues on its long journey to the coast at Flamborough. You should continue heading roughly north towards York Grounds Farm and a minor road from Raywell to Riplingham.

Turn left along the lane for a hundred yards or so, then pick up a public bridleway which crosses a broad ridge of Howe Hill before descending to the eastern edge of Socken Wood. Here we again join a major track running east- west, and our way lies to the right, heading east for the village of Skidby.

The route along here is easy to follow, and can be very muddy underfoot, but shortly the going becomes better as a rough, hard-core track is picked up as it passes beneath the old Little Weighton railway bridge at Rush Hill. The track passes Westfield Farm half a mile before coming to the outskirts of Skidby. This village is described in greater detail in Chapter Ten, although perhaps I should say here that the Half Moon pub at the eastern end of the village is definitely worth visiting, if only for its monster Yorkshire puddings!

Turn left at the Little Weighton Road in Skidby, and, as that road swings again to the left and climbs uphill to Ralph Nook, take a public footpath which heads north beside a mixed hedgerow. This path emerges onto the Dunflat Road near the site of the medieval village of Risby. Turn left along the Dunflat Road for 400 yards, until a

Nearing the end of the Beverley 20. The Minster from the Westwood.

public bridleway heads off north towards Risby Park Farm. This follows a good track underfoot, and the farm is soon behind as you cross a field on a tarmac lane heading for Halfpenny Gate Cottages. Just prior to reaching the cottages, a path leaves the lane and heads east around their back gardens. Follow this for 200 yards to a gate on the left which gives access to a nice little meadow, resplendent with stands of larch, beech and chestnut trees. In the centre of the meadow is Walkington Plantation, a decaying copse of mixed trees, and an obvious path passes this plantation to the left.

Our path soon joins another at the far corner of the field and heads straight for the outskirts of Walkington. Upon reaching the back gardens of the houses on the southern limits of the village, turn right and follow the public footpath beyond the edge of the village and out onto the minor road which takes infrequent traffic from Bentley to Walkington.

Turn right down this road. After a little less than half a mile, a track leaves the road on the left at Bentley Park and heads east. This is Moor Lane, and soon it enters a small wood known as Johnson's Pit near a slight 'S' bend in the track. As you leave Johnson's Pit another public footpath can be picked up heading north towards the Beverley to Walkington road near Broadgates Farm. Follow this, turning right at the road until you have crossed the A1079 Beverley bypass via a road bridge. Immediately after the bridge, a track leaves the road on the left and runs parallel to the bypass. Following this public bridleway, pass the murky western end of Swadgery Mere Wood, from where a public footpath heads east onto the common land of Beverley Westwood.

Walk across the open ground of the Westwood, passing clumps of gorse and thickets of hawthorn, towards the old Black Mill which stands in the middle of the common, being watchful for carefree golfers. From the Black Mill head south-east, crossing the Walkington Road, a minor lane which heads into Beverley, and pick up the next, busier road, the B1230, or Keldgate Road. Follow this into Beverley, continuing along Keldgate to the Minster. The Beverley 20 officially finishes at the north door.

To date it is known that 10,000 people have completed the Beverley 20, or at least that is the number of badges that Mr. Hood has issued to those that have informed him of their completion. It is, however, very likely that thousands more have actually done the walk and not thought to apply for a badge.

For those with yet more energy, Mr. Hood didn't stop at Beverley when it came to planning walks in the East Riding. He devised a further three walks, all of around 20 miles each to take the walker on to the coast at Filey. These walks are known as the Hutton Hike, Rudston Roam and the Headland Walk respectively, the whole 80 miles going under the name of the East Riding Heritage Way. Now that really would be a truly great walk. Parts of the Hutton Hike and the Headland Way are included in Chapters Nineteen and Seven of this book respectively.

Chapter Six

Walking around Welton

The pleasant little village of Welton, just off the north side of the busy A63(T), is well known locally for a number of reasons. Apart from the popular Green Dragon Inn where the walk starts and where the notorious highwayman, Dick Turpin, is reputed to have been arrested in 1739, the village has a cruciform church which dates back to the 15th century and has in its graveyard the body of Jeremiah Simpson, who had eight wives. Wonderful views across the River Humber stretch into Lincolnshire as far as the less well defined chalky Wolds of that county, and a delightful stream flows through the village of old houses with red pantile roofs, over-shadowed by the thin penduline [drooping or weeping] branches of willows, giving a delightfully rural air to the whole village and its environs.

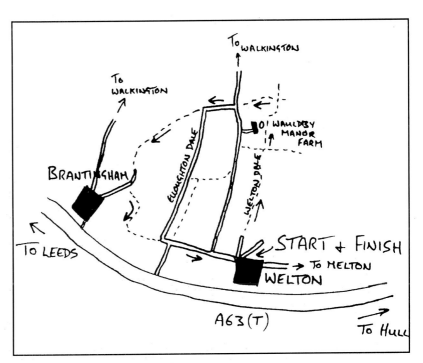

Our walk from Welton is about seven miles long and should take around three hours to do.

Parking near the Green Dragon, walk north-east along the lane with the gurgling stream on your right. Mallard and the occasional tufted duck paddle the shallow waters and weeping willows bend gracefully onto the shimmering levels. After a hundred yards or so, there is a crossroads, with the main lane swinging around to the right and making for the next village, Melton. The narrow walled-in lane on the left heads towards Elloughton Dale or to Walkington via another junction, while the lane straight ahead takes you through more of a residential area on a long dead-end road, or cul-de-sac, into Welton Dale. Take this latter road.

Through a white gate on the right after a hundred yards is the Old Stables where a small raised culvert diverts water through a little spout. Outside the gate, a notice on the wall reads:

'The Ancient Rights
of User of the
Cattle Well
and Overflow
Within These Gates
May Be Exercised
at Users' Risk.'

Within a few hundred yards of the Old Stables the track leaves the houses of Welton behind and goes through a gate which is usually left open, just beyond the old Welton Mill. The beck on the right runs parallel

The Cattle Well at the Old Stables.

to the track, draining the old Mill Pond which is hidden away in the willow trees on the right. The track passes over a bridge, where a stream from a smaller lake on the left, known as Welton Springs, joins up with the one on the right, just before a cottage beside a white kissing-gate. Pass through the gate and continue into Welton Dale. Plantations of young spruces, larch and firs are growing upon the gradual rise to the left, whilst the hillside to the right is open pasture land, dotted here and there with thorny, yellow-flowered gorse bushes.

The path stays in the dale bottom throughout, bending around to the left, but soon it enters Welton Wold Plantation via a gate and gradually climbs uphill towards a collection of cages on the left used as a breeding ground for pheasant and other game birds. Though the pheasant is a universally well-known bird of the countryside, it is not actually a native of Britain. Its real home is the Orient. Legend has it that it was first introduced to Europe by Jason and the Argonauts around 1300 BC. They brought it back from Colchis (hence its Latin name

The Green Dragon Inn at Welton.

Phasianus colchicus) on board the *Argo* on their return from searching for the Golden Fleece. Some zoologists, however, maintain that the Romans were almost certainly the first to introduce the bird to the British countryside around 50 AD, while others claim that the Saxon invasion was the first likely introduction of the genus.

From near the cages the path continues straight ahead for a short distance before entering a much more open thicket of beech and sycamore trees. Again the path climbs gradually, finally reaching a concrete drive leading from a minor road to the left, to Welton Wold Farm up on the right. Turn right onto this drive and climb uphill for a couple of hundred yards until a long narrow wood heads across the field on the left. A footpath runs along the right-hand side of this wood towards Wauldby Manor Farm.

At Wauldby is a large farm and small collection of cottages based around a pond, though there was once a much larger hamlet on the site, each house being built at very different historical periods. In 1835, Mr. Charles Howard found buildings at Wauldby that were 'old, ill-constructed, and have been erected at different periods, with a view of supplying the present want, but without any attention to regularity of plan or regard to general convenience'. A small disused chapel survives among the present buildings.

Continue roughly northwards, passing the pond and buildings on their right side, before bordering fields on

St. Helen's Church
in Welton.

an obvious track. This section of our walk is also part of both the Wolds Way and the Beverley 20, and is very popular with walkers.

After a short distance the bridleway bends round to the right and then back left around Turtle Hill. Just beyond these bends another junction is reached, where you should turn left. Again the track passes through a long narrow wood, known locally as Bottom Plantation, before emerging at the minor road which connects Welton with Riplingham. Almost opposite the point where the track joins the road, another minor road heads westwards before eventually turning south and descending into Elloughton Dale. Follow this road, but, just as the road turns to the south, take the wide farm track straight ahead, soon passing beside Long Plantation.

This track soon runs into a tarmac road and should be followed until it swings round to the right and drops steeply downhill to Brantingham. From this point a public footpath leads through a wood on the left. Following this, you soon reach another track which crosses ours at a T-junction. Turn right here, as the left-hand turn leads onto the private property of South Wold House.

Just around the next bend a path drops into the valley on the left whilst another continues through the wood after a short bend right. Take this track around the bend. Walking through the tall beeches of Scarbro Wold Plantation, you are now not far from the magnificent Victorian house of Brantinghamthorpe Hall with its vast estate. Continuing through the old beech wood you are soon faced with a marvellous panoramic view across the Humber into Lincolnshire. Even staunch Yorkshiremen will have to concede that this view really is one of the best to be had from anywhere in the East Riding!

The path bears left and gradually descends via a narrow avenue of bramble thickets to the foot of Elloughton Dale where the minor road that we crossed higher up the dale, beyond Wauldby Manor Farm, takes a sharp turn left. After closing the gate behind you that leads through onto this road, go straight ahead and take the minor road around the southern flank of Elloughton Hill all the way back to Welton, a distance of about a mile. Although I am not a fan of road walking, I always enjoy this section of the walk for the superb views across the river.

To the west a great curve of this wonderful estuary takes in the wildfowl refuge of Whitton Sand, before the Rivers Ouse and Trent merge at the point of Faxfleet Ness. At the convergence of these two rivers lies the Royal Society for the Protection of Birds Reserve of Blacktoft Sands, well-known, quite apart from its huge diversity of wildfowl and waders, as one of the few regular winter sites of that beautiful scarce raptor, the hen harrier. This medium-sized bird of prey flies low, quartering the ground when hunting for food, chiefly small mammals, especially mice, but also small birds, insects, snakes and lizards. The adult male is easy to spot and identify, being a light grey colour on the top of its wings and its back, and pure white underneath. The females and young are predominantly brown, streaked below, but with a prominent white rump (a bar at the point where the tail joins the body).

To the east the towering supports of the Humber Bridge, the world's longest single span suspension bridge, dominates the view. Beyond the bridge, the River Humber curves gently in a south-east direction, before flowing into the deep waters of the North Sea at Spurn Point. A really magnificent view from the southern termination of the Yorkshire Wolds. A bench beside the road gives a good excuse for a rest, and the best place to appreciate the huge volume of water that pours down from the mountains of the Pennines far to the west. Some of England's mightiest rivers flow out to the sea through the Humber, including the Trent, Don, Calder, Aire, Wharfe, Nidd, Ure, Swale, Derwent and, of course, the River Hull. In fact, it is said that the Humber drains a fifth of the country's watershed.

Chapter Seven

The Flamborough Headland Walk

Flamborough Head will always be a favourite spot with walkers, holiday makers and naturalists alike, and quite rightly so. Few visitors would come to this area without walking at least part of the Headland Walk, and certainly few of those that do could fail to be impressed by the dramatic sweep of vertical chalk cliffs, plunging almost shear into the boiling waters of the North Sea far below. The plethora of sea birds which come to nest here are also a real crowd-puller, with razorbills, gannets, puffins, cormorants and guillemots battling against the many species of gull, both for air-space as they wheel above the waves, and for nesting space on the tiny ledges which adorn the cliff face. It is no coincidence that Flamborough Head has been designated a Site of Special Scientific Interest, and since 1994 as a Sensitive Marine Area. On an international scale it is being considered as a Special Area of Conservation, a designation that will make it part of the European network of protected sites known collectively as Natura 2000.

Our walk of around 12 miles will follow the very rim of these high cliffs, and so extra care is needed. There are rescues here every year, and not all of them conclude with a happy ending. It should be noted that parts of this walk have been affected by landslides recently, though well-marked diversions are in place. Permanent alterations have been planned for the future by the East Riding of Yorkshire Council.

The walk starts in the bustling sea-side town of Bridlington, which marks the northern-most extremes of the boulder clay cliffs which form the whole of the coast from Spurn Point northwards. However, beyond Bridlington, as the coast bends

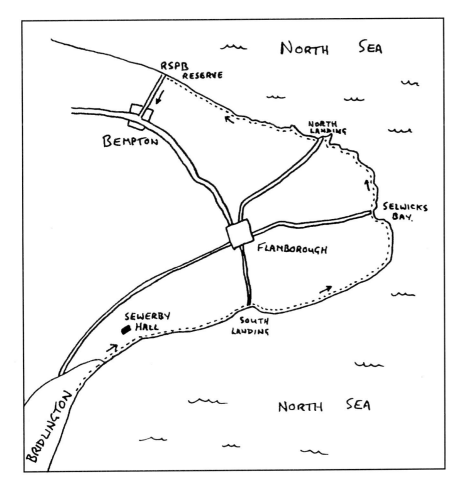

The old lighthouse on Flamborough Head.

the best place to start is the railway station, as our walk actually ends at Bempton, and, unless you can arrange a lift from there, it will be necessary to return to Bridlington by train.

A number of signs, aimed at both the pedestrian and the motorist, lead to the sea front, from where you should turn to the north, and begin walking towards the outskirts of the town along the promenade. Soon the cliffs begin to rise and a lane leads beyond the village of Sewerby to a path beside Sewerby Hall Gardens. These are open to the public, and have a small zoo, an arboretum and beautifully landscaped walled gardens.

Beyond Sewerby the scenery becomes more impressive as it leads on to the wooded trough known as Danes Dyke. From here you enter the inner sanctum of the village of Flamborough. Indeed, being quite effectively cut off from the rest of Britain to the west by the trench of Danes Dyke, the village is almost like another country. It is no coincidence that the headland is also known as Little Denmark. Many of the older inhabitants speak a language somewhere in-between English and Danish. It is true that this headland was once colonised by the Danes, although it has been proven that Danes Dyke was dug long before they arrived, probably during the Bronze or even the Stone Age.

Our path continues around the lip of the cliffs, leading along the coast to the bay known as the South Landing. Here is a car park and visitors centre, just above the point where the road drops down to the shore at a little sandy cove. From Flamborough village itself you can enjoy a shorter walk by following the road on foot to the South Landing Lifeboat Station, then walking around to the North Landing and so back to the village. From the South Landing climb up wooden steps to gain the cliff top, heading east.

A broad path follows close by the edge, eventually passing a cluster of detached chalk seas-stacks [detached pinnacles of rock, formed by coastal erosion] around

around the headland of Flamborough Head to the north-east, the rock structure changes to that of chalk, and this promontory forms the termination of the Wolds landscape, jutting for six miles out into the North Sea.

There are many parking places in Bridlington, though it can get very busy during the summer months. Perhaps

Selwicks Bay, the one in the very middle of the cove going under the name of the Eve Rock.

The lighthouse dominates the sky-line hereabouts, with its flashes out to sea of the letter 'H' in Morse Code. All of our coastal lighthouses flash a different sequence to aid navigation for shipping, as each chart of British waters marks the correct sequence of flashes for each lighthouse. Anyone approaching from the sea will have a reasonably good idea of which area of the chart they are in, and, seeing the lighthouse flashing 'H', can then look on the chart to find which it is, take a bearing, and so work out their exact position.

Half a mile further inland along the road which leads from the village down to the light-house (the B1259), stands another white tower. It is known locally as the Old Lighthouse, Beacon Tower or Danish Tower, although it is known that it was never used as a lighthouse. Some authorities give 1674 as the date of its building, but it is known that in 1326 Sir Marmaduke Constable obtained authority from Edward III to crenellate his manor-house at Flaynburgh, and some believe that it could date back to that reference. Whenever it was built, it had probably been used as a beacon before John Matson built the more modern lighthouse nearer to the cliff top in 1806.

Our walk continues north-west around the coast, alongside a golf course. The cliffs still plunge away to the right, and form the end of our only range of hills in the East Riding – the Yorkshire Wolds. Although these hills

Flamborough North Landing, where the Yorkshire Wolds end abruptly at the North Sea.

are not dramatically high when compared to other areas of Britain, if you have enjoyed any of the walks from this book already, I am sure you will agree that they do provide excellent quiet walking in beautiful surroundings.

Passing Stottle Bank Nook, Cradle Head and Breil Nook, another mile and a half beyond Selwicks Bay brings you to the North Landing, perhaps the most spectacular cove on this walk. Great waves have carved passages and caves into the chalk, and three in particular are well known: St. George's Hole, Robin Lythe's Hole and Smuggler's Cave. They can be explored at low-tide by taking the slip-way down to the beach alongside the Lifeboat Station. Do remember that the tide here comes in remarkably fast, and many people have had to be rescued. The caves themselves are a favourite roosting place for a variety of differing bat species, and many sea birds also nest among them and along the cliffs.

Wonderful escarpments of chalk continue around to the west, and a good path follows along the rim. More stacks, where arches have been formed by crashing waves and finally collapsed leaving unsteady pillars of white rock masked by green and black guano, stand bravely against the elemental seas, and gannets, puffins, cormorants, shags and rock doves fill the air amid screeching herring gulls and the seemingly quieter great black-backed and black-headed gulls. Many of the sea-stacks along the whole of the Headland have been given names such as 'Adam and Eve' or 'The King and Queen', although 'The Queen' no longer stands.

Soon, the path re-crosses Danes Dyke and the cliffs rise higher above the tumultuous sea. This is Bempton Cliffs, possible the most famous Royal Society for the Protection of Birds Reserve in this part of the country. Not only do thousands of sea birds flock here, but there is always a strong possibility of catching a glimpse of any number of other, much rarer birds. Short-eared owls can be seen on the coarse-grass hillsides around the Reserve, and, on my last visit, small flocks of Lapland buntings

and snow buntings were in the area. Snow buntings are usually only seen in the Highlands of Scotland where they spend the summer, but the winter brings them to the lower ground of our coasts, and large flocks can occasionally be seen. The Lapland bunting is much more scarce. It breeds in Arctic Europe, but again spends its winters on North Sea coasts, often flocking with other small birds and making it very difficult to identify. On one visit I met someone at the Reserve who had driven all the way from Northamptonshire on the off-chance of seeing a Lapland bunting.

There is a visitor centre with a small gift shop and displays, and there is always someone on hand to give you advice. The best time to visit for the sea birds is May and June when they are nesting and young chicks abound, though even at other times of the year there is always something interesting to see.

At Bempton Cliffs our journey around the Headland finishes and we must head back inland to catch the train back to Bridlington. The access road for the Reserve is quiet, apart from the odd car full of bird-watchers, and leads within an easy mile to Bempton village.

Not so very long ago, the men-folk of the village used to descend ropes down the cliffs to collect birds' eggs from their precarious nests. The spectacle was a familiar sight and people came from miles around to see them being lowered down the sheer walls. This, of course, has now been stopped, as all birds' eggs are protected by law.

The village itself is small and composed of many twisting ways and narrow lanes. Traces of pit-dwellings of an Ancient British village have been found in the area.

A quarter of a mile south of Bempton, along a minor road, lies the railway station. There are trains back to Bridlington, but these can be infrequent so it is as well to check before leaving home. Taking this into account, you should allow a good six or seven hours to complete this walk. This will give time to explore the caves of North Landing if the tide is out.

Chapter Eight

Walking around Warter Wold

The quiet little village of Warter straddles the B1246 road from Pocklington to Driffield, about midway between Pocklington and the village of North Dalton. It lies on the course of the old Roman road which ran from Brough to Malton, a road which can still be traced in part to this day.

Well-known for its quaint thatched cottages which surround the village green and its former stately home known as Warter Priory with over 300 acres of rich woodland and farmland, it is the ideal place to begin a walk. Warter Priory itself was the home of a number of well-known families over the years, but alas has now been demolished. In its early days it was known simply as Warter Hall, but around the 1830s it was renamed. Beside St. James's in Warter village is the site of an Augustinian priory, founded in 1132, and the larger scale Ordnance Survey maps show the extensive earthworks of this, the original Warter Priory, overlooking Golden Valley to the north of the village. In 1899 a gravestone was discovered which was engraved with the carving of a prior. Unfortunately, nothing is visible of this original priory today.

The original Warter Hall was built in the late seventeenth or early eighteenth century by the Pennington family, later to take the title Lords Muncaster of Cumberland. It remained in its original state until the 1860s when much external work was carried out, altering the style of the house. In 1878, the fifth Lord Muncaster sold the house, by then known as Warter Priory, to Charles Wilson of Hull.

St. James's Church, to the north of the main road, may look to be very old, but was actually rebuilt in 14th-century style in 1862 by Lord Muncaster. It is now a redundant church owned by the Yorkshire Wolds Buildings Preservation Trust. Shortly before the sale of Warter Priory to Charles Wilson, Lord Muncaster also undertook extensive work improving the houses of the village.

Members of the Wilson family, of the line which later became known as the Ellerman's Wilson shipping line, who once owned the Priory, are commemorated in fine monuments and stained glass within the church. It was Charles Henry Wilson, the first Lord Nunburnholme, who inherited the world's biggest

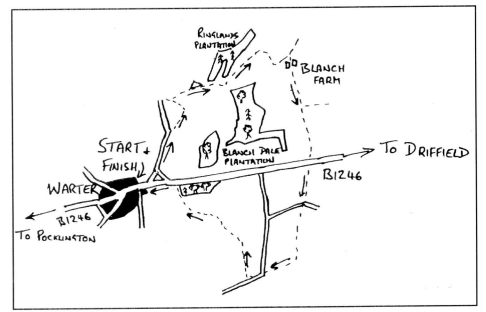

privately owned fleet of merchant ships from his father, Thomas, and was without doubt one of the most successful citizens of the city of Hull. He is commemorated by a life-size statue at the junction of Lowgate and Alfred Gelder Street in the centre of Hull.

Charles Wilson died in 1907, but his wife continued to live at Warter Priory until her death 20 years later. In 1929, the house was bought by the Hon. George Ellis Vestey, son of Baron Vestey, who kept it until his death in 1968, at which time it was bought by the Guinness Family Trust. Shortly after, the contents of the house were put up for auction, along with the garden statues and other small fittings. Everything was disposed of by May 1972, and Warter Priory was demolished the same year.

Most of those who remember the house bemoan the loss of its magnificent gardens rather than the building itself. It is usually remembered as an eyesore, a rambling monstrosity, and totally unmanageable.

To the east of the church and village green stands the village duck pond opposite Bucksey Bridge, beside the Hunger Hill lane to Loaningdale. The pond is attractively set, though never has much in the way of wildfowl on its waters. In winter, vivid burgundy branches of the red dogwood form a frame around the pond with a frieze of evergreen ivy as a back-cloth. You can leave your car here to start the walk. Just to the east of the pond, a lane turns off the main road on the left and makes for Huggate via Minningdale, the head of Scatter Dale and the Mill Lane

Thatched cottages clustered around the village green in Warter.

30

of Huggate village. Warter itself has its own Mill Lane which runs south-west from the village green, turning sharply over Washdike Bridge on its way to Nunburnholme.

Our walk, however, starts along the lane to Huggate, in total is around eight miles long and should take about four hours to complete. Walking steeply uphill along this lane, which climbs the broad nose of Scarndale Hill between high hedgerows alive with tiny passerines [generally any perching bird species], you come to a public bridleway which soon leaves the road at a point where the road turns sharply left. Follow this track, taking a left turn where it passes through a large gap in a hawthorn hedge.

Following the field boundary north-west, you meet another track which soon joins ours from the left, where we take a sharp right to contour above Three Corner Plantation on the northern flanks of Blanch Dale. The arable fields of Ringlands separate the bridleway from this mixed woodland.

Again, this is typical Wolds scenery, with chalky fields sweeping down into grassy dales, and playing host to a wide variety of animals and plant-life. Hares are probably the most common mammals that you are likely to see hereabouts, and a number of bird species populate the area. In winter, if you're lucky, you may catch sight of a buzzard wheeling against the sky. This is the largest bird of prey that you are likely to encounter in the Wolds, though even then it is a rare passage migrant or winter visitor. Its food source is predominantly small mammals such as shrews, voles and mice, and it can surely have little difficulty in finding a plentiful source in this region.

Possibly one of the most familiar birds of prey, not only in the East Riding, but also in the rest of the country, is the kestrel. At an estimated 100,000 pairs in Britain, it is by far the most numerous of our birds of prey. Indeed its nearest rival, the sparrowhawk, which can also be frequently seen in the Wolds, only numbers around 20,000 pairs in this country. Probably the most likely reason for this much higher population is that at one time birds of prey were persecuted relentlessly in Britain, Europe and North America, chiefly by the game-preserving fraternity. Though there is no doubt that the kestrel suffered great loses alongside its bigger brethren at the hands of these gamekeepers, the kestrel has the ability to produce large broods of chicks every year, including during its first year, so the recovery rate for the kestrel has been much faster than the other raptors of Britain. Another reason the kestrel is seen quite often is that it has a habit of hunting in the open, often along the verges of main roads and its characteristic hovering flight draws attention to itself. It is also quite an adaptable bird. Whereas the sparrowhawk suffered greatly at the loss of huge areas of forestry which have been cleared over the centuries to make way for sheep grazing and agriculture, woodlands being its main habitat, the kestrel came into its own on the more open land which it favours, and positively thrived.

The bridleway passes a couple of small modern woods of deciduous trees and underlying scrub on the left before dropping down into the beautiful Lavender Dale. Bulls often roam with the herds in these wild flower pastures, but are on the whole fairly docile creatures. From the bottom of Lavender Dale an obvious green track strikes across the hillside opposite, towards the left-hand skyline. There is an obvious track through the bottom of the dale, and, although you could follow it up the small valley towards Keasey Plantation, then gain the hillside on the right from there, it is not actually a public right of way, whereas the green track which climbs the hillside above the dale is. This track also gives good views down the whole length of this typical V-shaped dry valley.

Heading north-east the path contours above the grassy slopes of the valley, finally turning right between two hawthorn hedges near the head of Brig Dale. Within 200 yards a gate on the left gives access to another track which runs beside a wood towards Blanch Farm. The

Ordnance Survey map actually shows the footpath running along the south side of this wood, although in practice a public footpath signpost points along the northern edge, before passing through the wood into the farmyard. From Blanch Farm take the concrete drive which heads south-east over a slight rise known as The Meadows. This driveway is a public right of way and there are a number of ancient barrows in the fields along either side of this track. Just over a mile after leaving the farm you should cross directly over the B1246 and continue along the right side of a hawthorn hedge towards a minor road and distant wood. This track is not sign-posted but is a public footpath. At the minor lane, known as Middleton Road, the path continues southwards, initially alongside Middleton Road Plantation, a narrow belt of deciduous trees, then contours above Shipton Dale to the left. Another narrow belt of trees is soon reached and you should turn right here to follow the path along its northern edge.

This public footpath soon joins the minor road to Loaningdale near to the entrance to Farberry Garth Farm, and you should follow the lane westwards for a short distance until another path leaves it on the right beside a tall hawthorn hedge. The path from here is obvious as it follows the boundaries of Dugdale Fields high above the deep cleft of Great Dug Dale to the left. After a mile and a half the path runs through the western end of Townend Wood, a nice mix of deciduous and coniferous trees. The path is pretty straightforward at first, but, just before you gain the main B1246 road, it seems to come to a dead end at a fallen tree. The correct path is actually not very obvious here, and, if you retrace your steps for ten yards or so from the tree, you can just pick out a faint trod on the left which avoids the obstacle and gains the edge of the wood at the roadside. A stile leads out of the woodland and onto the B1246. Turn left and follow the road for 500 yards back to your car. Be careful of speeding traffic on this last section.

Chapter Nine

The Lost Villages of Cowlam and Cottam

The deserted village sites of Cowlam and Cottam sit in splendid isolation on the highest point of the Wolds to the immediate north of Great Driffield. The busy B1249 through Langtoft passes close by the latter to the east, while away to the west, across the grassy defile of the secretive dales of this part of the region, Cowlam lies within a few miles of Sledmere village. And yet few wander from the main arteries of the country – the Langtoft road to the east, the B1252 to the west and the B1253 to the north – in search of the beauty and solitude that is present in these hills for all to discover.

Do not be misled: these villages are only partially deserted. At Cottam there still stands the proud structures of Cottam House, Cottam Grange, and a little to the south the clustered cottages around Cottam Warren Farm, but the crumbling red-brick church, standing at the head of the dale, tells of a time when a thriving community lived out their lives here.

Cowlam Manor is often a hive of agricultural activity, but the church there, almost identical to the one at Cottam across the Wold, has also fallen into disrepair. The only other houses at Cowlam, apart from the few buildings at the Manor, lie along the minor road to the south at Low Cowlam, and there are a few way-side cottages at the crossroads just to the north.

When you drive around these quiet country lanes in this part of the Wolds, or walk the route described here, you cannot help but feel the immense quietude of these dales. But the very fact that communities, albeit much reduced from their former days, do still eke out a living from these healthy farm lands, and do play a part in collectively working for the good of that community,

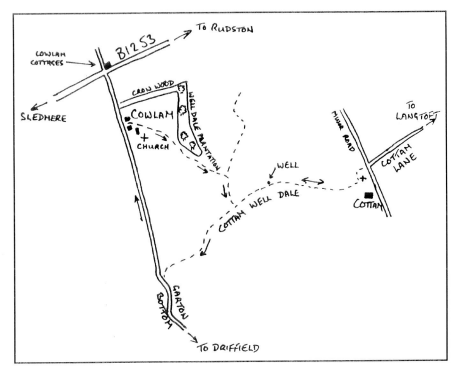

Map labels: TO RUDSTON, B1253, COWLAM COTTAGES, SLEDMERE, CROW WOOD, COWLAM, WELL DALE PLANTATION, CHURCH, WELL, COTTAM WELL DALE, MILLS ROAD, TO LANGTOFT, COTTAM LANE, COTTAM, GARTON BOTTOM, TO DRIFFIELD

leaves you content in the knowledge that there is still life to be found in this wind-swept corner of the Wolds.

This five-mile walk takes in these two villages via an ancient connecting path through the deep dales which lie in between. The walk starts at Cowlam Manor, but, as we return the same way after walking to Cottam, it is just as reasonable to start there and do the walk in reverse. From the B1253 heading east towards Bridlington from the village of Sledmere, a minor road turns south (right) after a mile and a half. This is at Cowlam Cottages, just beyond the farmstead of Collingwood at a cross-roads. Just over half a mile down this minor road, Cowlam Manor is reached on the left and a public bridleway sign points through the farmyard of shady trees and yapping dogs. Leave your car sensibly by the roadside, making

sure not to block access to any fields or buildings, and take to the bridleway.

Immediately the walk has interest, as the tiny bellcot church stands upon the rise to the right amid the barns and outbuildings of the farm. It was rebuilt in the middle of the last century and has little of architectural merit, other than once boasting a double-decker pulpit and a wonderful Norman font, elaborately carved in typical style.

There is little evidence of the Bronze Age encampment which once stood here, likewise the Roman road which led from Bridlington to York across these very fields, though over 10,000 Roman coins were once found in a field near the farm.

Of a later date in history, the village of Cowlam played a role in the English Civil War in the East Riding. In 1644 Sir William Constable of Hull's Parliamentarian forces regularly attacked Royalist forces from an encampment on the Wolds. In retaliation Royalist troops were sent from York to put a stop to Constable's military raids, and set up camp at Cowlam village (it has often been stated that this was at Kilham, barely six miles to the east, though it is now widely recognised that this was not the case). During the night, Constable's men crept into the camp and overcame the Royalist troops, taking 160 prisoners. It is likely that this all took place on the cold night of 10 February, a date which was followed shortly by Constable capturing Bridlington from the Royalists on 12 February. In those days military activity was often quick moving, despite the time problems

The deserted bellcot church at Cowlam.

associated with manoeuvring troops from one battle site to another. Other skirmishes involving Constable soon followed at Driffield and Helperthorpe, both by the middle of the same month.

Our way lies along a farm track, often muddy but easy to follow, which heads east from the farm. A fence to the right acts as a guide, and occasional fence posts have faded public bridleway signs tacked to them. Within a short distance a narrow belt of deciduous trees, known as Crow Wood, runs along the far side of a field that you should be nearing, and, at a junction of paths, you should take the one to the right, descending into the delightful dry valley of Cowlam Well Dale. The wood, now named as Well Dale Plantation, forms the northern side of this defile while the southern side is open and grassy, offering good grazing to the sheep that are often roaming these hills.

Well Dale Plantation itself has much of interest, though, being private property, you should stay on the right-hand side of the border fence. Pheasants abound beneath its leafy canopy, and titmice can be seen flitting from branch to branch.

During last winter (1998-99), a large influx of robins found refuge from the seasonal weather here. This is rather an unusual occurrence, as robins are pretty much considered to be territorial birds, rarely venturing from their own area. However, on occasion, the east coast of Britain is swamped with large falls of Continental robins on migration. There, they are less territorial, and towards the end of each year they make for warmer climes than their Northern Scandinavian summer homes. If adverse weather occurs over the North Sea at the time of the Continental robins' departure, many of these birds drift too far westwards, and we in Britain witness a population explosion. During late September and October of 1998 such conditions did occur, and ornithologists reported incredible numbers of robins as well as song thrushes off the east coast. In many cases these birds would have recuperated for a couple of days before continuing on their journey south, but many of them simply head inland in search of an alternative over-wintering site. It seems very probable that Well Dale Plantation was one such site. As I walked down the dale I counted at least 20 individual robins. A rather impressive count considering that I wasn't even stopping to see if I could see any more among the foliage.

The way continues down the dale, soon passing the end of the wood, where for a brief spell a fine stand of mature hawthorns cover the tussocky grassland that is the left-hand bank of the valley.

The public footpath signs hereabouts do exist, though in most places have faded, making it difficult to tell exactly in which direction the arrows are pointing. After leaving the small stand of hawthorns, you reach a fence with a gate leading into a field on the right. This is just before the wide side valley of Phillip's Slack comes in from the left. A stile can be seen crossing a fence and giving access to this dale, but should be ignored. Our footpath lies through the gate. An indistinct path follows a line of hawthorns along the main valley bottom, keeping the small trees to the left, before another gate leads at right angles into the much wider valley of Cottam Well Dale. Public bridleways head off in both directions from this gate, but we follow the one to the left, heading towards Cottam.

Incidentally, the path to the right, down Cottam Well Dale, brings the walker out at the minor road on which you have left your car, albeit a good two miles further

The upper regions of Cowlam Well Dale.

down the hill, but it is worth considering for a variation to the return journey, or as a shorter alternative for those not wishing to continue to Cottam. Once on the road near the head of Garton Bottom, near to where a remarkable Iron Age chariot was discovered buried in 1971, simply turn right and follow the quiet lane back to your car over the broad nose of Driffield Road Close.

However, the main way goes through the gate and turns left, heading up to the dale head. On the way you will pass the old Cottam Well, now covered with planks to avert any unnecessary accidents, but if you are careful you can take a peek into its depths. It does seem very deep, and I would hazard a guess at around 100 feet or more.

Hereabouts the dale is more open and grassy on both flanks. Soon, another set of twin gates in reached, and you should take the one on the right, remembering to close it behind you. This next field is often home to half a dozen ponies, a couple of which always seem to enjoy cantering up behind you, not veering away until the very last minute. Oh, well, they're only having a bit of fun!

Again the valley splits near its head, the way lying up the open dale to the right. As you turn a corner, the old bellcot church of Holy Trinity, Cottam, comes into view at the very head of the valley, above the old cultivated terraces of the village. This decrepit place of worship stands in a truly remarkable position on the slopes of Chapel Hill. It was built around 1890, but by only 1945 had fallen into disrepair and was abandoned. As you near it, a public bridleway sign leads around the field's perimeter to the left and onto an access track for the farm buildings to the south. This leads out onto a minor lane to the west of Langtoft, but, unless you have arranged transport to pick you up there, you should turn around and retrace your steps back to Cowlam, bearing in mind that there is a minor variation to Garton Bottom as described above. In all, you should allow two to three hours for this walk, which is ample time to enjoy the scenery and the natural history of this part of the Wolds.

Chapter Ten

The Woods of Risby Park

The village of Skidby, with its well-known pub ,the Half Moon, and its four-sail windmill standing as a landmark alongside the busy A164, is the starting point for this walk, a total of about six miles, with the option of taking a shorter return of around four miles. The village itself is a small collection of old and modern houses clustered around a 14th-century church set in a shallow fold of these south-eastern slopes of the Yorkshire Wolds.

From the northern end of the little street known as Church Rise, that is the lane opposite the church with a tiny chapel standing on the corner, a public bridleway known as the Oldgate heads off down the hill, through a short avenue of hawthorn trees, and soon crosses a grassy pasture before passing beneath an electricity pylon and on into a wood. This is an alternative section of the popular long-distance walk, the Beverley 20, and as such is well marked with familiar yellow 'Public Footpath' arrows, placed at intervals on gate posts and trees.

The path soon climbs out of a shallow wooded valley near its head via a narrow cutting on the left and gains a farm track beside the field boundary. Away to the north-east, the imposing twin towers of Beverley Minster can be seen beyond the chalky arable expanses of Platwoods Fields and Beverley Parks. Being on the very eastern edge of the Yorkshire Wolds, the flatlands of the Holderness Plain sprawl far out towards the coast in that direction, holding in their foreground the massive sprawl of the City of Hull, while, to the west, the small rounded hills and deep-cut valleys of this long chalky ridge rise gently in arable slopes towards the High Hunsley radio mast.

Within three quarters of a mile the path takes a sharp turn right, passes a couple of young rowan trees, each with deeply incised ash-like leaflets and vermilion berries,

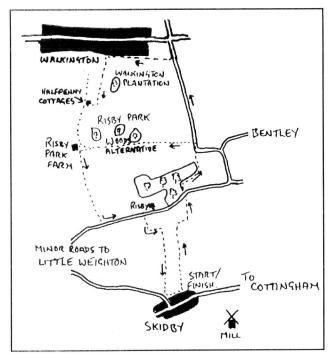

then turns left and comes out at the narrow lane known as Dunflat Road.

Almost opposite, another footpath sign is marked as 'The Beverley Beaver Trail' and points down an alley of hawthorn hedge and barbed wire fence with the dark canopy of Fishpond Wood to the left. (The Ordnance Survey map actually shows another thicket to the east of the path, naming it as Folly Wood, and marks the public footpath as heading deep into the trees on Old Moor before taking a sharp right to come out onto the fields beyond the woods. In actual fact the path merely skirts around the edge of Fishpond Wood, and Folly Wood doesn't exist at all where the map places it.)

In the midst of the private, broad-leaved Fishpond Wood lie a number of small, man-made freshwater ponds, popular with coarse fishermen, who must pay a fee for a day's fishing there. Older maps show Folly Wood to the immediate south of the larger of the two main lakes, and a Gothic octagonal folly still stands near its banks. The woodland itself is in the process of being thinned out, and, on my last visit, much of the undergrowth of brambles, saplings and other brash had been cleared. Following the path around the perimeter, you take a sharp turn left leading along a straighter section atop Low Daw Hill to cross an overgrown ditch, before a gentle climb up to the minor road which takes infrequent traffic from Bentley to Walkington.

Heading north along this road for a hundred yards, you reach a footpath leading across a field to the left, eventually abandoning the middle of the field for the right edge beside a good hedgerow. This segment of land is known as the Hornsea Belts, and the path is the one to take as a shorter option to this walk. I will describe this four-mile circuit first, and then go on to explain the slightly more lengthy alternative.

The public footpath continues heading west, passing a number of small conifer plantations and compact thickets of deciduous species of tree, each plantation having its own wonderful sounding name. To the north of the path you will find Sodwall Plantation, Silver Fir Plantation, Broom Cover and Cupola Hill Plantation, whilst across the fields to the south lie Gorse Plantation and Blackdike Plantation. These woods are all private property, belonging as they do to the Risby Park Estates, though I for one would love the opportunity to explore their hidden corners further.

From one point along the southern boundary of Sodwall Plantation a hedgerow cuts across the field to a corner of Blackdike, and on numerous occasions I have seen the deep slots of a roe deer print in the mud heading alongside this hedge. As roe use the same runs from generation to generation, there is a strong chance that sooner or later I will come across a small family in this area, but I can't help but feel that I would have better

Skidby Mill to the east of the village.

on the map as a footpath) is a wide track going straight ahead. A couple of old footpath signs tacked onto a gatepost show that the landowner doesn't object to walkers using this short-cut.

At the point where this path emerges onto a good chalk track, just to the left of Risby Park Farm, the longer, alternative route joins this from the right and the direction of Walkington. From now on both routes are the same. Another alternative to a section of the Beverley 20 leads south and is signposted on the gateway to the left. Follow this track to join the minor road to Little Weighton. Earthworks are visible in the open grazing fields on the left, showing clearly the site of what is marked on current maps as the medieval village of Risby. In actual fact these are the remains of 17th-century Italianate terraces of the formal gardens of Risby Hall grounds. In 1540 Sir Ralph Ellerker had a house and small deer forest here, and is known to have entertained King Henry VIII. This house stood in the area known as Cellar Head, though that which is associated with the formal gardens was built for Sir James Bradshaw of Bromborough, Cheshire, in the 1680s on a new site nearby. During the 1770s and 1780s two disastrous fires blazed at Risby Hall, and, soon after, the house was demolished. The actual village earthworks of Risby lie nearer to the minor road just 200 yards from where the public bridleway joins it.

At the minor road, turn left and head back towards Fishpond Wood, which can be seen just beyond the collection of farm buildings at Risby. Before Risby is reached, just 200 yards short of the entrance to the farm, a footpath leaves the road on the right and heads south towards Skidby along the left-hand side of a stout hedge.

Along this part of the walk the Humber Bridge comes into view away to the south, with the dark low smudge of the Lincolnshire Wolds beyond. Nothing can be seen of the mile-wide Humber Estuary flowing beneath the bridge because of the convex nature of these southern flanks of the Yorkshire Wolds, dipping gradually to the

luck on this score if I were allowed to examine the woodlands in greater detail. Roe deer are predominantly woodland creatures, and only usually cross fields as a means of getting from one wood to another, or very occasionally in winter if food is scare on the trees or brambles that cloak the woodland floor. Only then will they give up their browsing habit and take to grazing for weeds and other leaves in the open.

Before long the path starts to descend into a small but obvious valley. The footpath shown on the Ordnance Survey map for the area heads diagonally across the field to the right, passing a copse around an overgrown pond on its way to a group of farm buildings at Risby Park Farm. Although this path does exist and is signposted, another more obvious alternative (although not shown muddy shore between Brough and North Ferriby. To the south-east the four sails of Skidby's windmill stand beyond the village, with the far distant view being dominated by the BP works at Saltend, beyond the sprawl of Hull.

Our path takes a turn to the left, and a sharp turn right through a gap in the hedge before continuing back to Skidby at the Little Weighton Road. From the road it is a simple matter to follow it round back to the car, or you can follow a public footpath along the northern boundary of the village to a leafy passage into Church Rise. And so to the end of the shorter variation of this pleasant little walk.

In order to extend the walk to take in the village of Walkington, you must follow the road from the top of Low Daw Hill, soon after leaving the edge of Fishpond Wood. After three quarters of a mile, atop a rise beyond Bentley Park on the right, a public footpath sign points across a field towards the west. The going is easy and soon has the houses of Walkington close by. Our path doesn't actually enter the village, but there are a couple of excellent pubs and a shop if you require refreshment.

The public footpath skirts around the southern boundary of the village, passing by the playing fields. I really do hope the residents of these houses appreciate the many tiny birds which rely on them for food during the winter months. The last time I walked this path I counted nearly 30 different species of bird, including various members of the tit, thrush and finch families. Sparrows were everywhere and even the odd treecreeper froze to the trunks of the larger trees as I passed.

Soon the path veers to the right near the church, but, just before that, another public footpath heads south down a broad alley formed by a fence and a hawthorn hedge. This leads out into a pleasant grassy meadow south of Park Farm, and the track swings around the western side of Walkington Plantation, an odd mix of enclosed elder, yew, beech and ash trees. Within half a mile a gateway leads onto a good track which climbs to the west to pass behind Halfpenny Gate Cottages. From the cottages, a tarmac drive leads south-eastwards to Risby Park Farm, from just beyond which our way rejoins the shorter alternative to this walk and on towards the Little Weighton Road near Risby.

The track from Risby Park Farm at the Dunflat Road. This track is also taken by the High Hunsley Circuit.

Chapter Eleven

Toeing the Path alongside the Pocklington Canal

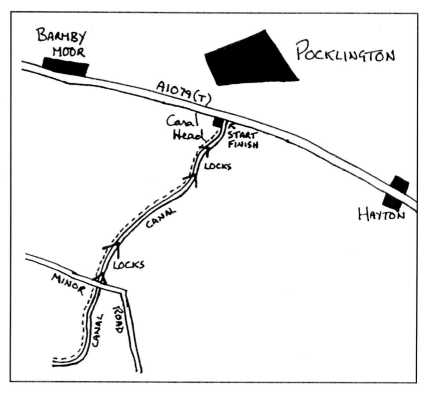

The lively market town of Pocklington lies 10 miles east of York, and just off the busy A1079 trunk road. Originally founded in Anglo-Saxon times by 'Pocela's People', hence its modern name, by the time of the Domesday Book (1086) it had risen to being one of only two boroughs in the East Riding of Yorkshire. Nestling into the tranquil green flanks of the western scarp of the Wolds, the town today has a number of claims to fame. Sadly, little remains of the old Norman church, the existing one being built during the 13th and 15th centuries, but perhaps the most historically exciting thing about the town is the old grammar school. William Wilberforce's ancestors settled in East Yorkshire long before his time (1759-1833) and took their family name from the nearby village of Wilberfoss. The young William, soon to become renowned for his part in abolishing the slave trade, studied at the 16th-century school in Pocklington. However, extensive rebuilding took place to the original school during the last two centuries.

The market itself became a popular trading post in the 13th century, but it was the building of the canal which was started in 1815 and opened in 1818, linking Pocklington with the River Ouse via the Derwent, and the later coming of the railway that transformed the place into the thriving town we find today. In all, the canal had nine locks and a set of steeply humped bridges taking minor roads, some of which are in the process of being lovingly restored by a local society. In 1848 the York and North Midland Railway (shortly to become the North Eastern Railway) bought the canal and began a gradual running down of operations on it. It finally closed in the 1930s.

Another popular attraction in Pocklington used to be the Penny Arcadia. This contained an amazing collection of penny slot machines ranging from the very old 'What the Butler Saw' to the more modern pinball machines. It was housed in the Ritz Cinema and described as 'Not so much a museum as a fun palace'. Unfortunately, it is no longer open.

Nearby you can see the world-famous collection of

water-lilies at Burnby Hall Gardens, said to be the largest collection of that order of plants (the Nymphs) in this country. The garden was bequeathed to the town by the late Major P. M. Stewart upon his death in 1962. It was once estimated that, together with the garden's neighbour, the Hayton estate, there are over a million trees growing in the vicinity, surely something to be proud of. Also within the grounds is an incredible summerhouse, made from a single log of a Big Tree of California. The tree is said to have been 200-feet high, and the dimensions of the summerhouse support this fact. It measures 15 feet in length and 38 feet in diameter.

Our walk, however, follows the tow-path of the now disused canal, although as the walk can be made as long, or as short as you like, you could easily make time to explore Pocklington and its environs as well. Another local attraction which is worthy of your attention while in the area is the nearby Allerthorpe Common and Nature Reserve. This is one of the few remaining remnants of lowland heath in the country, and plays host to a large number of plant and animal species, perhaps the most exciting or sinister, depending on your point of view, being the adder or viper. This is the only poisonous snake to be found in Britain, though it must be made clear that the adder only attacks when startled. The best time to view the snakes is on a balmy summer's day when they can usually be found basking on the heath.

The Reserve itself covers nearly seven hectares of heathland which is set within the much larger pine forest of Allerthorpe Common owned by Forest Enterprise. The Forest Enterprise acquired the land in the early Sixties, and by 1963 more than half a million trees had been planted. However, it was recognised that the small area that is the Reserve was especially important as a wildlife habitat and it was handed over to the Yorkshire Wildlife Trust to manage. It is now designated as a Site of Special Scientific Interest, and access to the Reserve is strictly by permit only. These permits are available from the Yorkshire Wildlife Trust offices in York (see appendix for address). The rest of the common is freely open to the public and provides a number of excellent woodland walks along wide forest rides and fire-breaks.

But now we begin our walk along the Pocklington Canal. A large car park at Canal Head, just off the A1079, near the popular Wellington Oak pub, once the Pocklington Canal Inn, is the start of the walk. The path is obvious throughout its length and so requires little in the way of detailed description, but is nevertheless a delight to follow. Simply leave the car park at Canal Head and follow the path along the western bank of the canal.

A series of four locks lead within a couple of miles to a hump-backed bridge taking the minor road from Bielby towards Thornton and Allerthorpe. This is about as far as many people will want to walk, as it is necessary to return the same way, but, if you wish, you can continue alongside the canal all the way to its confluence with the River Derwent at Wheldrake Ings, a National Nature Reserve near the village of East Cottingwith. Beside St. Mary's church in East Cottingwith there stands a headstone with an inscription to one of the region's most famous professional wildfowlers, Snowden Slights. The inscription reads simply:

'In Memory of Snowden Slights
Wildfowler
of East Cottingwith.
Born June 14th 1829
Died April 15th 1913.'

During his time Slights is known to have killed thousands of swans, geese, ducks and plovers with his huge punt gun on Wheldrake Ings, though thankfully this Reserve is now owned by the Yorkshire Wildlife Trust who manage the site sensibly as one of the most important wildfowl and wader wintering sites in the world. The towpath to East Cottingwith from Canal Head at Pocklington, however, is a good nine and a half miles long, and, unless you can arrange transport back to the start (public transport being notoriously fickle in this part of the world), it would make a very long return journey indeed on foot. Also worth bearing in mind is that, strictly speaking, only the section up to the hump-backed bridge near Bielby follows a public right of way, though there is a private track underfoot all the way to the Derwent.

However, the real attraction of walking the canal, certainly for me, has always been the wide variety of fish, insect, bird and amphibian life you are likely to see. Better to take your time and have a good old poke around in the water margins of common reed, great reedmace and other rushes, and also in the duck-weed which often covers the water. In the water itself it is not uncommon to see a number of freshwater fish species alongside common frogs, common toads, palmate and smooth newts. If you keep a watchful eye on all things alive in the water, electric-blue kingfishers can often be seen perched above on the thin branch of a waterside willow, whilst the grey heron gazes intently into the depths for hours on end, patiently awaiting the arrival of his next aquatic meal. Wheeling above the trees which line the canal bank, you might catch sight of the odd buzzard, sparrowhawk or kestrel. Mallards and their hybrids, along with the occasional pair of ringed mute swans, also grace the waters, while moorhens nod their way from bank to bank. This is one of the few places in the East Riding that I have also regularly seen the common lizard and its legless relative, the slow worm. This 1 to 2-foot-long creature superficially resembles a snake, but really is more closely linked to the lizards of the reptile world.

I have also walked this path once or twice during the last few winters, and even then have found much to see in the way of bird-life. Redwings, fieldfares, and other thrushes fill the trees and fields to either side of the canal, and on one bleak winter's day a pair of mute swans slid amusingly around on the iced-up waters on comically over-sized feet. Another circled overhead, looking for an open stretch of ice-free canal on which to make its splash-landing, but eventually gave up and headed off to the west, presumably towards the River Derwent.

The insects that abound in the area during the summer months are also fascinating. Apart from the well-known orange-tip and common blue butterflies which frequent all chalky Wold scenery, the air-space above the canal is usually buzzing with blue damselflies and the very rare red-eyed damselfly, virtually unknown elsewhere in Yorkshire.

All in all this path heading south-west from the Canal Head can take about as long to walk as you have time to spare. Whether you go for a quick stroll along the tow-path, or take a packed lunch and the kids out for a full day, you are likely to want to return here time and again to explore just that little bit further.

Chapter Twelve

Milling around Millington

The delightful Wolds village of Millington has long been a favourite starting point for walkers heading off for a day on the chalky hills nearby, or in the many deep dales around Millington Pastures, just up the valley. On any given day in summer, the minor road through the dale, known as Wood Gate, which runs on towards Huggate to the north-east, is a hive of activity with families picnicking, ramblers exploring the quieter corners of the area and day-trippers wandering through the broad-leaved woodland of the Millington Wood Nature Reserve.

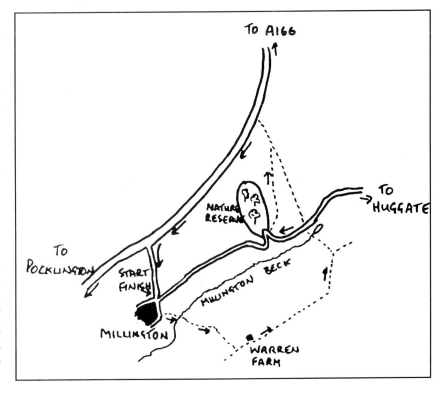

Even the long-distance challenge walks of our county seem to converge on the village and its environs. Both the Wolds Way and the Minster Way pass through, or very near to, the village centre, and the 20-mile-long North Wolds Walk (see the next chapter) sees regular streams of walkers plodding through the village.

After you have parked in the village centre, a muddy track leads eastwards down a gentle incline soon to cross the gurgling waters of Millington Beck. A stile leads to a short boggy section across the grassy meadow beyond, although duckboards have been placed to aid easier walking over this obstacle, before climbing steeply uphill towards Warren Farm on the skyline. The public footpath actually crosses the hillside diagonally, climbing steeply above the wide griff of Wan Dale, a subsidiary of this dry valley system, and now playing host to countless ancient hawthorn trees and the odd gorse bush, providing excellent cover for the many rabbits which live on the chalky slopes. The path, however, is indistinct when approaching from this direction, but a short distance over to the left lies a chalky access track to the farm, slowly bending its way up above Millington Bottom to join the footpath beside a stand of hawthorn trees near the edge of the more open pastures above.

As you gain height, the path heads to the right of the farm buildings, passes under a line of telegraph wires and squeezes through a hawthorn hedge. Turn sharp left here and follow the hedge round to pass just above the farm. This broad plateau of chalk is known locally as Cold Moor. Of course, the whole Wolds chain was once

A traditional Wolds hostelry, the Gate Inn at Millington.

nothing more than a plateau, but, following the last Ice Age, streams gouged out the many deep valleys, cutting the plateau into complex ridge and dale systems.

As the path passes the farm, it bends slightly to the right and the obvious track ahead goes out onto a minor road near a small reservoir. Before this point, however, a Minster Way sign points into the middle of a small elderberry thicket, under-grown with thick clumps of stinging nettles. A large gap in the hedge to the left gives access to a broad arable field with a hedge down the middle, along which the signpost appears to point. Stick to the left side of the hedge, following it round as it descends slightly to the left high above the open slopes of the upper valley known as Becks. Crossing over a stile, the public footpath leads into a grassy pasture above the middle part of Sylvan Dale, resplendent with spiky gorse, and, usually, a large herd of inquisitive cattle. The broad nose of chalk, falling on the left down to the valley bottom where Sylvan Dale and Millington Dale converge, is known locally as Rabbit Warren. It was here that back in the 17th and 18th centuries the local farmers used to encourage the breeding of rabbits, both for food and for their fur. This was a widespread practice, and one that can be traced to hundreds of other sites throughout the three Ridings.

At the bottom of Rabbit Warren, as you descend into Sylvan Dale, pass down through the hawthorns and milling cows, and walk down the dale. Just before crossing a small pond in the Millington Beck, usually barred by a gate, cross a stile on the right and follow the path down a narrow gap between a high hedge and a barbed wire fence. A small wooden bridge leads over the beck and out onto Wood Gate, the minor lane running through Millington Pastures.

If you have time, it is worth walking left along the road down the dale for a quarter of a mile to explore the well-maintained Nature Reserve at Millington Woods. This excellent example of an ash woodland flanks the side of Lily Dale below a minor ridge called Lammas Brow. The wood was recorded in Domesday Book (1086), described as a pastoral woodland known as Lilling Dale. A number of locally rare species of flora thrive in the wood, including the wood anemone, lily-of-the-valley and bane berry. On a national scale Millington Wood is important as the habitat of the very rare toothwort.

The wood has been owned by a number of individuals and groups during its known history, including William di Perci, Robert de Brus and the Constable family. The Constables of Flamborough took over the land through the marriage of William Constable to Isobella Brus in 1220, and kept it as part of their estate until 1562 when it was willed to St. John's College, Cambridge, along with the Manor of Millington, in exchange for the right for four scholars to be maintained at the college. The college duly leased the manor and the wood to a number of tenants, and letters dating back to those times, sent as correspondence from the tenants to the college, give the current owners a good indication of what the management structure of the wood would have been over the last couple of centuries.

The traditional uses for the timber felled in Millington Wood were for building, fencing, furniture and charcoal burning. At last, in 1956, Millington Wood was recognised as an important site locally and was designated as a Site of Special Scientific Interest by the Nature Conservancy Council, now known as English Nature. In 1959 the wood was sold by St. John's College to the Forestry Commission, who embarked on an intensive management programme. Only a small area of this ancient ash woodland, so characteristic of the type of forest that would have once covered much of these chalky Wolds, was left untouched by the Forestry Commission.

In 1985 an offer was made to the Forestry Commission for the purchase of Millington Wood by Humberside County Council. Grant aid from the Nature Conservancy Council and the World Wildlife Fund helped to smooth the way, and in 1991 Millington Wood was finally given the status of a Local Nature Reserve, the very first in Humberside. The East Riding of Yorkshire Council now owns the site and has appointed a Countryside Ranger for Millington Wood.

If time is pressing, however, you can leave a visit to the Nature Reserve for another day. Our path goes straight across the minor road and follows an ancient paved path steeply uphill, known as the Thieves' Spy. This runs along the site of a Roman Road towards the top of Garrowby Hill, where the remains of a Roman fortress and the Temple of Diana have been unearthed. To the south, the Roman road can be traced climbing up the hillside of Rabbit Warren, then heading south-east via Coldwold Cottages to the village of Warter and on, to its ultimate goal, the Roman camp of Petuaria, now known as Brough.

After the steep climb up the Thieves' Spy, open field systems around the First Heights bring the buildings of Millington Heights Farm into view. These are passed by closely to the right, continuing until the top of Givendale Hill is reached. Soon after, the minor road coming down from the A166 towards Pocklington is underfoot and, turning left, you should follow this for about a mile and a half along the long southern ridge of Givendale Hill. Names hereabouts are given on the map in plenty, though, sadly, many of their origins are no longer traceable. On this ridge we find the High Barn fairly self-explanatory – I'm sure you will agree – but what about Lammas Brow and Sugdel Top? At Balk Pit we find another road leading off to the south-east and back downhill to the village of Millington and the end of the walk. This delightful lane is known simply as The Balk. Back in Millington a good pub, the Gate Inn, and a 'rambler friendly' café give a good excuse to linger a while after your exertions, although in total this pleasant walk is only about 4½ miles long and should take no more than about two hours to complete. That is, unless you decide to make a day of it by carrying a packed lunch and paying a visit to the Nature Reserve.

Chapter Thirteen

The North Wolds Walk

This 20-mile-long walk takes in all that is good about the Yorkshire Wolds and you should allow a full day to complete it without feeling rushed. With deep chalky dales to explore and sleepy picturesque villages to discover, walkers from all over the region return to these northern Wolds time and again, especially as many shorter variations of this challenging walk are possible. One or two are detailed in this book, and, where the chapters share the same public footpaths for the odd short section, I have refrained from repeating any unnecessary information.

Heading east from Stamford Bridge on the A166, the main road climbs steeply up Garrowby Hill, passes a radio antenna and the summit of Bishop Wilton Wold, the highest hill in the Wolds chain, then descends barely perceptibly to a junction with the minor road to Huggate within just a mile. Here, hidden behind a bank which screens a picnic site from the speeding traffic, lies the Wayrham Car Park. This is the start of our walk.

From the car park at Wayrham, the North Wolds Walk follows the road towards Huggate, passing over cross-roads and on, until a lane branches to the left. Opposite this is the bridle-way which leads downhill into Greenwick Dale and on through the mixed woodlands of Great Plantation (the same way as taken in Chapter One of this book). Ignoring two paths which join the main track on the right, cross a stile and leave the wood behind, continuing down Frendel Dale until you meet a narrow road in Millington Pastures. Cross this and a steep, signposted path can be seen on the left of a hawthorn hedge. Climb up the hill on this path, passing Jessop's Plantation before dropping down to the grassy Nettle Dale. Climbing up the opposite hillside above Cow Moor, ignore the obvious chalk track on the right-hand side of the fence, taking the faint path up the left. At the top of the hill the path borders a field before crossing another stile, then goes very steeply down to the Rabbit Warren in Sylvan Dale. This section follows part of the route taken in the previous chapter, although in the reverse direction.

On the hillside over to the left, a stile can be seen. Head straight for this, crossing over it, then follow the edge of the field before gaining the track heading for Warren Farm along the Minster Way. Turning downhill just after reaching the farm will lead you along a public footpath which curves downwards into Wan Dale and on to the village of Millington. At the final bend in the track a stile can be seen down in the valley bottom. Aim for this, crossing over the infant Millington Beck before entering the village and the chance for a refreshment stop at the Rambler's Rest.

Heading north-west out of the village on the minor road known as The Balk brings you to a T-junction at an old quarried site known locally as Balk Pit. Opposite the junction is a public bridleway which will take you down and through the delightful Whitekeld Dale. The Whitekeld Beck which flows passively along the dale bottom drains Bishop Wilton Wold to the north. This section has some of the best scenery of the entire walk, passing numerous small ponds before reaching the tiny candle-lit St. Ethelburga's chapel at Great Givendale. The minor road opposite the chapel, known as Givendale Lane, is again part of the Minster Way which soon takes a right turn down a track and onto the open Garths End Fields above the West Pasture and South Cliff. Being on the very western fringe of the Wolds gives an unsurpassed view over the wide Plain of York to the distant smudge of the

Walkers enjoying a stroll through Great Plantation.

Pennines. Follow the Minster Way along the field edges to eventually drop down to a minor road which heads north to the village of Bishop Wilton.

Upon reaching Bishop Wilton, leave it again almost immediately by taking Park Lane on the right. This soon becomes a muddy track leading through a gate into an open tree-fringed grassy pasture, known as Milner Wood. A signposted path wanders across this and up the hill, before contouring around the valley head. The path passes above the mixed woodland scrub of the Old Wood before eventually reaching a small conifer plantation above Worsendale, known as Crow Wood. This plantation should be kept on the left before dropping downhill for a short distance. A path on the right contours

above the head of Worsendale and is enclosed on both sides by wire-fences. This public footpath soon leads out onto Worsendale Road, a short section of minor road which should be followed uphill to reach the busy A166 at the top of Garrowby Hill. It is perhaps worth mentioning here that those who may be finding the going tough should take this opportunity to call it a day. Many miles lie ahead with little in the way of short cuts, whereas it is a simple matter to follow the A166 eastwards for just under two miles to reach the car park at Wayrham. If taking this option, be very wary of the busy road and its speeding traffic.

Straight across this road is a good farm track which passes through Cheese Cake Wold on its way to Kirby

Underdale via Megdale Brow and the western edge of Megdale Plantation. If continuing with the North Wolds Walk, follow the lane northwards through this small hamlet, taking a right at the second junction and on towards a bridge over Waterloo Beck beside a cottage with the same name. The road continues to the hamlet of Uncleby, but our way lies across the fields of Wood Leys to the north, following a public footpath from a point just a hundred yards from Waterloo Cottage.

Cross over Jenny Wren's Spring and pass Wood Leys farmhouse on the right in the bottom of Open Dale. A track heads north, then following footpath signs heads east, steeply uphill, skirting the farm close by on the right.

This section is quite a long uphill plod, and can be tiring at this stage in the walk. At last the top is reached at a point where a stile is crossed into the mixed wood of Northdale Plantation. Once over the stile, follow the field boundary to the north from where signposts lead out onto a minor road. This follows the course of the Roman road which ran from the old Petuaria, now known, of course, as Brough on the banks of the Humber Estuary, to Malton. Just north of here the Roman road must lose height dramatically as it leaves the Wolds at Leavening Brow to descend to the flat, arable plains around the Derwent in the Vale of Pickering.

A short distance north along this road, a chalky farm

The tempting Cross Keys Inn at Thixendale towards the end of the North Wolds Walk.

track on the right leads to Thixendale Grange. From the Grange a gate on the right gives access to the long meandering valley of Milham Dale, which eventually takes you to the sleepy village of Thixendale.

A couple of small shops, petrol station, pub and youth hostel combine with the few houses and converted barns to give Thixendale a nice peaceful atmosphere. The village is named from the six valleys which meet here, although some believe it is perhaps more likely that the first settler here was a Viking called Sigsten.

From Thixendale the lane heading south should be followed past three left-hand junctions, and on until a perfect V-shaped valley appears on the left. This is the upper valley head of Thixen Dale, a classic dry valley of the Wolds, with the exception of Bradeham Well further up the dale. Countless streams from other minor dales once fed the main beck along the valley bottom, and, though nothing can now be seen of these, the deep-cut valleys that they formed join Thixen Dale at various points along its length and all have wonderful sounding names: Breckenholme Dales, Worm Dale, Pluckham Dale and Bradeham Dale.

From the road follow the numerous Wolds Way signs through the valley until a point where a path comes down from the head of Worm Dale on the right and a Wolds Way sign points abruptly uphill to the east. Ignore the sign and continue along the valley floor. Soon the valley again splits into two; this is the junction of Pluckham Dale to the left and Bradeham Dale to the right. Follow the dale bottom of the latter, passing Bradeham Well en route. The path passes through a short conifer wood owned by the Forest Enterprise Group before emerging in a clearing at a point where two more valleys join. These are Wayrham Dale on the left and Fordham Dale on the right. This time take the left-hand one through another small wood, then climb easily back to the A166 and a well-earned rest at the car park.

Chapter Fourteen

Filey to Scarborough – a Coastal Path

The town of Filey is either widely seen as one of the most attractive and idyllic spots on the whole of the Yorkshire coast, or else just another seething mass of holidaying crowds and day-trippers. This latter is hardly a fair description for such a charming town. Narrow streets lead down to the Coble Landing with its fine sandy beach on the sweeping bay, hemmed in to the northern, seaward side by the finger of gritstone known as Filey Brigg, and at a distance of six miles to the south-east the headland of Flamborough. This seascape encompasses all that is beautiful about the Yorkshire coast, and, personally, I love Filey and its environs.

The town itself has its fair share of history. It is known that a Roman signal station stood on Castle Naze, the cliff top above the Brigg. Filey Bay was shown on Claudius Ptolemy's map of Britain, drawn up a good hundred years before Caesar came. Carved stones believed to have been part of a Roman lighthouse have been found and a Roman pier is known to have been here.

Much of St. Oswald's, the Norman church, which 800 years ago belonged to the canons of Bridlington, still stands to this day, and Charlotte Brontë visited it during her stay at Cliff House. Of the church she wrote in a letter home:

'It is not more than three times the length of the parsonage, floored with brick, the walls green with mould, the pews painted white, but the paint is almost worn off. At one end is a little gallery for the singers, and when they stood up they all turned their backs to the parson. It was so ludicrous I could hardly help laughing.'

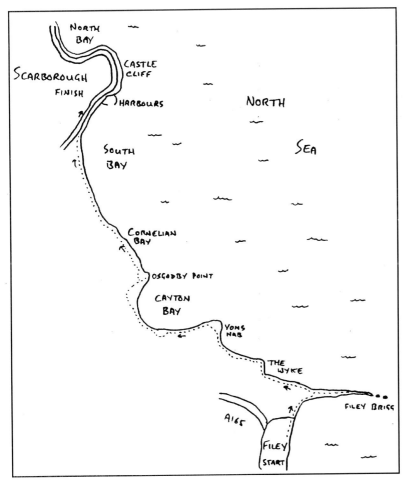

services linking the two towns (check times before setting out).

From the railway station follow road signs for the North Cliff Country Park. From a point near the entrance, a minor road leads down a wooded valley called Church Ravine to the Coble Landing, and you should either follow this or continue to a narrower track through another wooded valley known as Arndale, which leaves the Country Park at the first big car park on the right. There is usually a charge for parking at the North Cliff Country Park. Perhaps a better bet is to park at the railway station and walk through the town.

There are other ways of reaching the beach from the town centre, and many people will want to explore thoroughly before heading off for Scarborough.

From the beach, walk north to the Brigg. Here can be found rock pools full of anemones, starfish, crabs and various species of seaweed. From the Brigg gain the cliff top by a rough path up the steep slopes then follow the Wolds Way signs along the cliff edge.

This is the last stage of the long-distance walk that we have encountered a number of times already in this book. The path passes the coastguard lookout station before continuing along the top of North Cliff, with the bouldery beach of Under Nine Rocks at its base. Passing Club Point we come surprisingly to the end of the Wolds Way. I say surprisingly because it appears to finish in the middle of nowhere. Surely the logical termination of this long-distance walk would have been Filey Brigg? However, at this precise point the Wolds Way joins up with another long-distance walk which ends here, the

The town is also steeped in smuggling history. On Queen Street there is a house with a model of a ship above the door. This is known as T'Awd Ship Inn and was a regular meeting place for smugglers from the town.

As this walk of around nine miles follows the coast northwards to Scarborough, it will be necessary to arrange transport back to the start from Scarborough. The railway provides a good means of doing this with fairly regular

The impressive gritstone nab of Filey Brigg from Castle Naze.

Cornelian Bay replete with low-tide rock pools. An explorer's paradise.

wonderful Cleveland Way. This path of 109 miles follows a rough course around the western, northern and eastern perimeter of the North York Moors National Park, and we shall follow part of the Way into Scarborough today.

In all, these long-distance footpaths link up to provide the serious walker with a truly remarkable journey. It is quite possible to begin a walk at Great Yarmouth on the coast of Norfolk and to follow the Weavers' Way north through the Broadlands to Cromer. There you pick up the Peddars Way which takes you to Thetford and onto the Hereward Way which runs westwards through Peterborough to Oakham. The Viking Way then leads north to the Humber Bridge, from where we meet our old friend the Wolds Way. From just north of Filey the Cleveland Way takes the walker on to Helmsley,

The harbour and South Bay at Scarborough.

from where we can follow the Ebor Way to Ilkley and so pick up the Dales Way to Bowness-on-Windermere. In all a total of around 725 miles without leaving official long-distance footpaths! It is doubtful if anyone has ever followed this course, but, if so, they would have completed an incredible eight long-distance paths. That is roughly three times the length of the Pennine Way!

For the time being, however, we will concentrate on getting to Scarborough. Our way leads around the cliff top throughout and so really requires little description, though the series of small headlands, or Nabs as they are called hereabouts, keeps up the interest level until the very end. First, we curve around The Wyke, an open cove, before rounding Cunstone Nab. Flat beds of rock are scoured by the crashing tide as it rises and falls on the right, while to the left the ground falls away gently to the Carrs and Ings of the Vale of Pickering. To the south of the Vale rise those familiar hills, the Yorkshire Wolds, while to the north the hills are higher and heather-covered – the hills of Cleveland and the North York Moors National Park.

We pass caravan sites on the cliff edge above the ragged beds of Old Horse Rocks, Casty Rocks, Castle Rocks and Calf Allen Rocks below Gristhorpe Cliff, as guillemots, puffins, little auks and razorbills throw themselves from the heights into the foaming waves in search of fish. Gannets, white in their adult plumage, or mucky grey as juveniles join the throng, as do cormorants and shags. The shag is also known as the green cormorant and many people experience difficulties telling the two species apart. While they are both very dark, in fact, almost black, the cormorant has an obvious white patch on its face and another just above its leg. It also has a much thicker bill and is noticeably bigger than the shag. During their first year the young are much paler, the cormorant having a white belly, while the shag is more of a 'buffy' colour.

After Calf Allen Rocks below the Nab of Lebberston

Cliff, a promontory known as Red Cliff Point, an open sandy cove is reached. This is Cayton Bay, from where the cliffs beyond, towards Scarborough, rise high in wooded slopes to Osgodby Point.

Next we come to Cornelian Bay, so named after a type of stone that is found there, usually known as carnelian. It is a variety of chalcedony or a microcrystalline type of quartz. In colour it is brown or cherry-red and has a dull but transparent distribution of colour caused by iron oxide intrusions. Also to be found are agates, another type of chalcedony but with a banded effect. Another gemstone that the diligent may find on these beaches is jasper, yet another form of chalcedony coloured by iron oxides into red, brown or black samples. Of course, you must be aware of the times of high tides before venturing down onto these beaches in search of stones and gems.

Also in Cornelian Bay can be seen huge numbers of waders. These birds flock to the bay in winter and numbers of some species can be spectacular. In January's of recent years counts have been made of up to 700 oystercatchers, 300 purple sandpipers and 200 turnstones. The bay is also favoured by sea ducks such as eiders, and common and velvet scoters in winter.

From Cornelian Bay we are nearing the fringes of Scarborough. Cleveland Way signs point across the top of the cliffs around the Black Rocks to bring the walker onto the Esplanade, a wonderful lane above the Spa and South Bay. The town itself is a sprawling mass of tourism, though that shouldn't deter the visitor from enjoying the sea front, the harbours around the South Sands, the excellently situated Castle with its remains of a Roman signal station and Marine Drive which takes you around the base of Castle Cliff and into the North Bay.

After a good nine miles of walking, taking four or more hours to complete if you have been waylaid along the route, signs lead into the town centre and so to the railway station with its links back to Filey.

Chapter Fifteen

The High Hunsley Circuit

This is by far the longest route in this book, and as such will be seen as something of a challenge by those who attempt it. Throughout its 25-mile length it continuously passes through some of the very finest scenery on offer to the walker in this part of the world. The High Hunsley Circuit was devised by the Area President of the local group of the Ramblers Association, Mr. Dennis Parker, as a training walk for long-distance challenge hikes such as the Fellsman Hike in the Pennines. The inaugural walk was on 4 August 1984, and a grand total of 16 members of the East Yorkshire and Derwent Area Ramblers Association – Beverley Group completed the circuit.

For the most part the route is very well marked with public footpath signs, following as it does, parts of the Beverley 20 and the Wolds Way. Only a short section from near Bishop Burton to Newbald Lodge is off public rights of way, but the East Riding of Yorkshire Council has arranged access across these fields. Along with supplying details of the route, for which I am grateful, Mr. Parker also pointed out that this part of the walk actually follows roads awarded by Inclosure Acts, and follows part of the old horseback route from Sancton to Beverley, and, as such, should actually be public rights of way. This will take years to clarify, but for the time being the route is open to the public regardless of this.

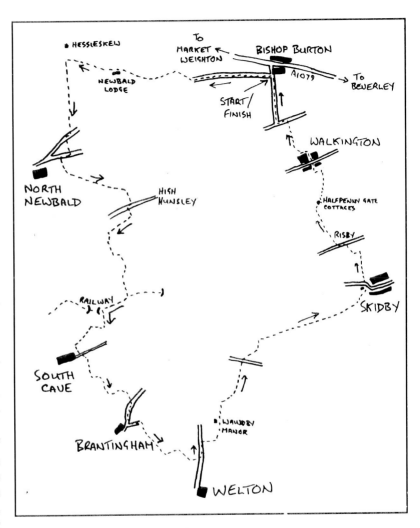

Being a circular walk, the High Hunsley Circuit can be started anywhere on the circuit, and the traditional place to start was always Walkington, although Mr. Parker suggests Bishop Burton, as parking is easier there. Of course, you should feel free to start at any point, and I would personally recommend either Skidby or

The Altisidora at Bishop Burton.

Brantingham. However, for the purposes of this book I shall describe the walk from Bishop Burton. The village straddles the A1079 between Beverley and Market Weighton, and lies just two miles west of the former.

There is a good pub in the village, the Altisidora, but, as you will be struggling to finish this walk within 12 hours, you should save that hostelry for a celebratory drink afterwards. Besides, in order to avoid walking in the dark, it will be necessary to start very early in the morning, long before the pubs open.

From the centre of the village make your way past the duck pond with its ever-present flock of mallards and greylag geese, and walk westwards, passing a Wesleyan chapel on the left, At the end of the lane turn left onto Finkle Street and by the last farm on the right, turn right onto Low Balk Road. This is a narrow, dead-end lane with few cars, and, although the first mile and a half follows this, it is a delight, passing through the typical Wolds scenery of woodland and arable fields around Bishop Burton Wold.

The way climbs steadily, then descends to a little col before climbing very stiffly up to the top of the Wold. Beyond a plantation known as Wellfield, a public bridleway sign points diagonally across a field to the right, and, although the way does go across the middle, the official route suggests continuing along the road for a further 300 yards and following the field boundary northwards towards Lings Farm.

At the next corner the bridleway heads west along the north side of another field boundary to the southern edge of Deepdale Plantation, a narrow belt of scrub. The way then leads north again, further into the denser cover of the plantation, passing it by on the right. At the point where the edge of the wood turns back east, the path heads west across the open fields toward Newbald Lodge.

Passing to the north of the Lodge, another agreed path heads west again to pick up a good track, and on to a minor road south of Hessleskew Farm. This minor road takes a sharp turn to the north at the point where the High Hunsley Circuit joins it, and the path leaves it almost immediately, following Wolds Way signs southwards. This track is easy to follow, heading south all the way, beyond Gare Gate, and on to pick up a minor road atop Newbald Wold. Here, turn right for 300 yards, then left along another track. This brings out at a further road upon which you should head westwards for another 300 yards.

A public footpath sign points south, and the way leads around a bend and down into the dry valley foot of Swin Dale, a truly pastoral part of the walk. A concrete dew-pond, which is passed half way down the dale, is the only water in the entire valley above Becksies, a series of springs by the side of the Newbald road. The site is owned by the Yorkshire Wildlife Trust as a good example of freshwater springs and their associated flora on a calcicole soil.

The way climbs gently to the head of Swin Dale and passes to the east of Whin Hill before gaining a field boundary in the narrow upper part of the dale. Here the path turns to the right, and then almost immediately to the left to gain a track that heads south to a minor road near North Plantation.

Still following the Wolds Way, turn right along the lane to a crossroads, passing straight over these and on until a signpost points south alongside a field boundary to another road, the B1230, which takes fairly regular traffic from Walkington to North and South Cave. Cross straight over this road and across fields until the edge of Low Hunsley Plantation. This is a delightful part of the walk, dropping down into East Dale as finches and tits flit among the branches of the mixed woodland trees.

Further down the dale another path joins ours on the left, coming down from Hunsley Dale, but our way continues on down the slopes until the line of an old railway track is reached in the valley bottom via a series of steps cut into the embankment. This was the route taken by the Hull to Barnsley line, opened in July 1885. Soon after opening, however, the owners found themselves in direct competition with the North Eastern Railway which was able to lower its charges considerably, and the new company fell on hard times. By 1921 an inevitable merger came and the line was kept open until 1959.

Our way follows the railway westwards, until a path climbs the hillside to the left, just before the line of the railway plunges into a short tunnel. This tunnel is a pretty grotty place to explore, and is private. I do remember in my younger days, however, when I first began discovering the Wolds on foot, walking through the tunnel and down into Drewton Dale. I can still recall the hoards of Daubenton's bats clinging to the roof, and I am told that it is still used as a favourite roost of this winged mammal.

The path climbs south from near the mouth of the tunnel, up the hedge-lined slopes of Comber Dale to emerge into a chalky track. Here turn right for 400 yards, then pick up a footpath heading south beside the eastern edge of South Cave village. This ancient village lies on the course of the old Roman road from Lincoln to York, although this path is as close as we get on the High Hunsley Circuit.

At the end of the path turn left onto a narrow lane and right again at a track which climbs up onto Great Wold. Footpath signs point south from here to pass around Mount Airy Farm and on to a path which skirts the edge of Woo Dale Plantation.

Heading downhill alongside the wood, the path crosses a spring, and a sign tacked to a tree points the way to the eastern side of Woodale Farm. A track through a meadow then climbs eastwards to a stile which gives access down into a sycamore wood and onto a minor road leading south to Brantingham.

Follow this road south until just past the church and a beautiful line of estate cottages. Here a public footpath leaves the road, just a few hundred yards short of reaching the village proper, and climbs steeply uphill to the edge of Wandhills Plantation and a minor road. Follow this very steeply uphill.

Where the road eases off, a kissing-gate on the right leads into a sycamore wood and the path continues to a muddy track above Elloughton Dale. Turn right along the track; then almost immediately a footpath sign points down into the dale on the left. The path bends around to the right, passing a couple of tree boughs that provide handy benches for those in need of a sit-down, and out onto the minor road in Elloughton Dale.

Slightly to the left along the road, another kissing-gate

A perfect setting for the church in Brantingham Dale

leads into another woodland of beech and sycamore and the path climbs steadily round in a gradual curve to a junction of paths at the top of the hill. Take the one to the right, but ignore another which turns right again almost straight away. The correct path keeps almost level here, and is the same path as was taken in reverse in Chapter Six. Continue out to the minor road above the western side of Welton Dale and turn right for 400 yards or so until a concrete road on the right drops down into the head of the dale. Keep the woods of Welton Dale to your right and follow this road until a narrow belt of conifers on the left lead across the fields to the north to Wauldby Manor Farm.

From now until Walkington the High Hunsley Circuit follows the same route as this part of the Beverley 20, and so I have refrained from repeating the directions. Basically, you should head north for York Grounds Farm, then on to Skidby, heading north from there to pick up the Dunflat Road just west of Risby. Way-markers are in place throughout and lead on to Halfpenny Cottages and around the western side of Walkington Plantation to bring you out at the path which skirts the southern boundary of the village of Walkington.

Here the Beverley 20 turns right and the High Hunsley Circuit turns left. Pass by the church and take the first lane on the right, crossing the B1230 for the second time today. The lane heads up past the Dog and Duck pub, but soon Manorhouse Lane turns off this road and heads back west.

Turn down Manorhouse Lane until an obvious kink in the road, from where a sign points north across the fields with a hawthorn hedge to your right. Follow this to another minor road, and turning left, look for a lane on the right. This leads in less than a mile back to Bishop Burton and a well-earned pint in the Altisidora.

Anyone who has completed this superb walk within twelve hours can apply to Mr. Dennis Parker for a badge. His address is given in the appendix.

Chapter Sixteen

Around the Castle Howard Estate

The estate of Castle Howard is surely one of the best for walking in this part of the country, the Howardian Hills, and I make no apologies for including it in this book. True, the range is separated from the Wolds by the River Derwent, but likewise it is separated from the North York Moors by the wide carr-land of the Holbeck valley and Ryedale and so does not really belong to those hills either. The Howardian Hills are a separate range in their own rights, but as such often suffer by being left out of books describing the Wolds, the North York Moors or the Yorkshire Dales. Few of the walks here have been described in print, but that is something I hope to remedy by including three in this book. To my mind the Howardian Hills fit in admirably with the other walks described within these pages, and, besides, they can all be reached easily from a base anywhere within the East Riding.

In 1692, Charles Howard succeeded to the title of third Earl of Carlisle, and during his life went on to become Gentleman of the King's Bedchamber, Earl Marshall of England, First Lord of the Treasury, Privy Councillor and Constable of the Tower of London. In those days, it was fashionable for the aristocracy to reside in grand country houses attached to large hunting estates, and Charles was no exception. When his castle and the adjoining estate of Henderskelfe village became damaged by fire he began planning a much grander house in the area to the south of the North York Moors, the area that today is known as the Howardian Hills.

After falling out with Talman, who had designed Chatsworth House, Charles Howard made the unusual step of commissioning a total novice to design what was to become Castle Howard. John Vanbrugh had been incarcerated in the Bastille, and upon his release had fashioned himself as a rather successful playwright. While

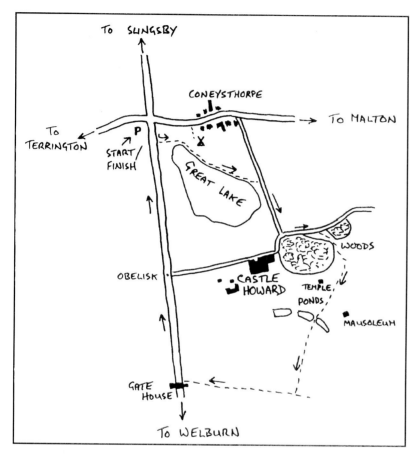

To SLINGSBY

CONEYSTHORPE

To MALTON

To TERRINGTON

P

START / FINISH

GREAT LAKE

WOODS

OBELISK

CASTLE HOWARD

TEMPLE

PONDS

MAUSOLEUM

GATE HOUSE

To WELBURN

a fire broke out. Two-thirds of the south front were destroyed, as was the huge dome, which had been the largest on a private house in the whole of England.

An extensive rebuilding scheme was mounted under George Howard, later to become Lord Howard of Henderskelfe, and the dome was totally restored along with the other fire-damaged rooms. In 1981 he added the impressive Garden Hall and two years later the Library, both built from original designs by John Vanbrugh. Of course, to most people these days, Castle Howard will always be known as the setting for the TV series *Brideshead Revisited*.

While our walk doesn't go too close to the Castle, it circumnavigates it from a car park to the north-west, and the main buildings are always in view.

A minor road heads westwards from Malton to the village of Coneysthorpe, which lies near a junction of another road which heads south from Slingsby on the B1257 Malton to Helmsley road. This cross-roads lies just to the west of Coneysthorpe and here you should turn south and park in a muddy lay-by to the right, beside a stone cottage.

Castle Howard lies to the south-west and has as its foreground the splendid stretch of water, the Great Lake. Although there is no public access to the lake, the estate has provided a permissive path around its northern shore, starting across the road from the car park.

A kissing-gate gives access to the path, which is often muddy at this stretch, and passes by clumps of bullrushes and behind a small thicket of trees. The area surrounding the lake is good for viewing a wide variety of bird species,

Vanbrugh's imagination was to play a large part in the eventual design of the house, the architectural skills of Nicholas Hawksmoor were brought in to keep things in order.

Financial constraints meant that by the time of Vanbrugh's death in 1726 the west wing was still unbuilt, but building continued under the watchful eye of Sir Thomas Robinson, brother-in-law to the fourth Earl. Various alterations continued through the following centuries, but disaster struck on 9 November 1940 when including green and great spotted woodpeckers and hawfinch, along with the more usual woodland birds, while the lake itself holds large numbers of ducks and geese. During my last visit I counted a total of 16 great crested grebes, as well as a few male goosanders and five cormorants. Also in attendance was a Slavonian grebe, a rare winter visitor to this country. The reed beds beside the shore, particularly those in front of the house, are a favourite spot for reed buntings, reed and sedge warblers, and the odd bearded tit, while grey herons watch carefully for passing fish. These large stork-like birds are not the only fishermen that you are likely to see, as the whole lake-side is popular with anglers.

The path follows the banks of the lake closely, passing by a large caravan and camping site on the left. There is no public access onto the site, other than for those staying there, but, as you come to the far end of the lake, with the imposing north side of Castle Howard glowering down at you from across the shining levels, you come to a public footpath which has headed south from just outside Coneysthorpe. It is worth remembering this path in case the permissive path around the lake is ever closed. It starts 150 yards to the east of the Coneysthorpe War Memorial.

Once on the public footpath, head round to the right towards a good deciduous woodland. Upon reaching the wood, follow a good estate track to the left and look out for a public footpath which leaves this shortly on the right and heads south around the edge of the wood beside a stone wall.

Beyond the wood the way continues around the eastern side of the Temple and makes for a fine stone footbridge which spans a lake. Away to the east lies the Mausoleum, once a favoured breeding site for ravens. These huge birds of the crow family are now very rare indeed in Yorkshire, and are hardly ever seen at all, never mind staying long enough to breed.

Once over the bridge head south to pick up a good farm track and here turn right. Follow the track to the

Castle Howard across the open parkland to the south-west of the Great Lake.

Gatehouse at a minor road. The Gatehouse spans the road via an arch and here you should turn right again onto the dead straight road and follow this back to the car park at the north-west corner of the Great Lake.

This road follows a fine avenue of deciduous trees, and, shortly after the Gatehouse, an obelisk stands in the centre of the tarmac. Here a side road leads to Castle Howard itself, and a sign tells you whether it is open or not. If so it is definitely worth the extra walk to view the house and grounds, a walk that is little more than a quarter of a mile each way. Note that the house is not open every day of the year, though, and that on some days only the grounds will be open. There is also a small plant centre here that is open more often than the house itself.

Although I am not a fan of road-walking, finding that the constant stream of traffic that whizzes by at close quarters is a bit off-putting, this last stretch of the walk back to the car park is a real pleasure. In summer there will inevitably be plenty of cars, but, for the walker, the avenue is blessed with very wide verges upon which you can stride out. At one point the way passes over a bridge which spans a series of small ponds, and beyond, the open fields on either side of the trees often have large flocks of greylag and Canada geese over-wintering in them.

Like so many other walks in this book, the walk around the Castle Howard Estate is only very short, around four miles, and the fit could hurry around it in a little over an hour. However, I have walked this route on numerous occasions, sometimes by slight variations, but have never managed to get back to the car in less than three hours. There is always simply far too much of interest to see, and those visiting the house itself could easily spend a full day here.

However long you take, and at whatever time of year, I can guarantee that the Howardian Hills will soon become one of your favourite stomping grounds, and that you too will return here time and again.

Chapter Seventeen

Around Thixendale

As far as walkers go, the village of Thixendale must surely rank among the most popular of places in the entire East Riding. Six major valleys converge here, and many believe that it is this characteristic that has given the village its name, though countless others radiate out from these dry dales to form a spider's web of chalky culverts, steep-sided in the extreme. The village nestles among these chalky dales, and in the now infrequent harsh winters Thixendale is among the first of the region's villages to be cut off. Ploughed fields are few, until you have gained the plateau-like Wolds that rise in every direction, though agriculture plays an important role in the lives of the village folk. Sheep roam the hawthorn-covered slopes, and many of the villagers' gardens have chickens or the odd goat chewing at anything that's edible, and the odd morsel that isn't!

There is a pleasant youth hostel here, a simple place where tired walkers can relax after a day on the Wolds Way which passes by the front door. The only fault I can find with this homely little shelter is that it is only open during the summer months, and that is invariably the time of year when I find myself walking or rock climbing in other parts of the country. To many locals the hostel is still known as the village hall, although it should also be remembered as the original school building.

A couple of cafés, a village shop and the Cross Keys Inn all go a long way towards making the travellers feel welcome, and indeed that is the general atmosphere felt by all who come here.

Thixendale lies a couple of miles to the north of the busy A166 and just to the east of the old Roman road from Lincoln to Malton. Actual derivations of the meaning of the name cannot be determined for sure, though it is now widely accepted that it is derived from the valleys which meet in the environs. However, Vikings raided much of eastern Britain after AD 793, when they made their first foray into this country at Lindisfarne in Northumberland. Norwegians settled much of Scotland, Ireland and the Isle of Man, while in England the Danes settled much of the eastern part of the country. By the year 880 most of East Mercia, as the whole of the eastern part of the country had been named by the previous invaders, the Anglo-Saxons or Mercians, was in the control of these Viking raiders, and some still believe it is plausible that Thixendale was so settled by a Dane called Sigsten, a fairly common Viking name. We shall never know for certain, but some find both theories to be equally appealing.

This walk from the village of Thixendale follows the ridges and valleys to the immediate north, but can easily be joined to the walk described in Chapter Four of this book by a short link path. This will give the walker departing from Thixendale the chance to explore the environs of Wharram Percy medieval village from a different approach, and brief details of this link path are included below.

Whichever way you approach the village to start this walk – there being a total of six roads into Thixendale, though not all of them follow the valleys – you should park towards the southern end of the village. By a little white-painted cottage, known as Round-the-Bend, a Centenary Way sign points down a side road, passing the village pub, the Cross Keys Inn. Resist the temptation to start off the day in there and continue past the door and a couple of other cottages on the right.

The main valley which holds the village is called Water Dale and you should continue down this dale into an open pasture with hawthorns growing high on an embankment to the left. A sheep track climbs gently up this embankment and you should follow this, aiming for a stile across a fence which is unseen at first, due to the convex nature of the terrain.

Once over the stile, the path leads

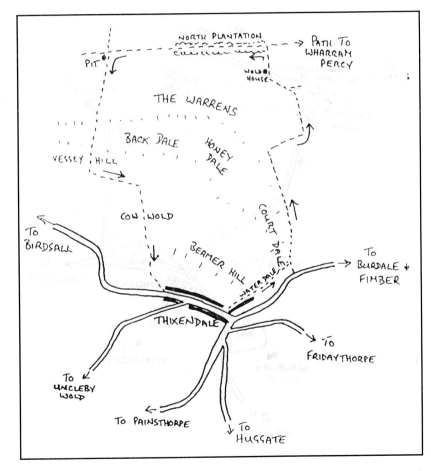

across the top of the grassy terrace upon which horse trials are often conducted, and, as you pass into the next valley, Court Dale, further horse jumps and fences can be seen along its length.

A confusing sign welcomes horse-riders to the valley, stating that it is called 'Six Valleys', though this is just an anglicised version of the name given to the whole area, not just this one dale.

Do not head up the dale, but cross immediately to a gate where another Centenary Way sign points up the chalky nab [a local term for a ridge or promontery] of the eastern edge of the dale. This climbs steadily to a row of hawthorn trees, which form a remarkable hedgerow, and contours along its lower side. The path is obvious and easy to follow, and being bordered to the left by occasional hawthorn trees as well as by the hedge

on the right, provides a good habitat for a number of birds which can often be seen flitting along in front as you walk.

In winter, mistle and song thrushes along with their close relatives, the fieldfares, redwings and blackbirds flock here in their hundreds and are guaranteed to cheer up any weather-worn walker. Summer also brings its fair share of our little feathered friends to the dale, and yellowhammers abound along with corn buntings, whinchats, redstarts, tree pipits and those doubtful members of the warbler family, the whitethroat and lesser whitethroat. I say doubtful because in general the warblers are widely considered to have the most delightful song of all birds, ranging from reeling trill to deeply melodic mimicry. Unfortunately, though the whitethroats do belong to that wonderfully harmonic

Thixendale, the perfect Wolds village.

Exposed banks of chalk above Vessey Pasture Dale.

family, their song can only be described as a hard and scratchy *tac-tac*.

Of the thrushes that we often see here, as well as in many other places in the county including gardens and parks, there is great concern for the song thrush among ornithologists at present. Numbers of these birds have declined dramatically over the last few years, and it is thought that mortality of young birds is the chief cause of this, although it has not been determined what exactly causes this mortality. The British Trust for Ornithology, the scientific equivalent of the RSPB, has collected reports from volunteers throughout the country showing that the most likely time for song thrushes to die is during the first 60 days of their lives. The BTO have placed the song thrush on the 'Red List' of birds of real conservation concern.

It is quite pleasant just to sit here among these

hawthorns in mild weather and enjoy the sylvan beauty of Court Dale from on high. As you continue along the path, more and more of the dale is revealed, and I always find it surprising that these dry valleys can be so long. In fact, many of the Wolds valleys lose very little height during their length, apart from the initial declivity at the very head of the dale.

At the end of the hawthorn hedge a lesser valley can be seen entering Court Dale from straight ahead, and our way passes well to its right. A gate passes through the hedge and the path heads north-east. At a chalky farm track you should turn left. The way passes over a shallow valley of scrub known as The Warrens before turning north to pass beside a ruined building, named on the map as Wold House.

This path heads for the eastern edge of North Plantation,

a narrow belt of deciduous trees. Here you should come to a T junction in the path. To the right the way leads above the upper flanks of Deepdale and on, northwards to Wharram Percy in just over a mile, while our way turns left and passes on the northern side of the plantation.

Soon a farm track comes down from the north and swings to the west, while our path reaches this corner and immediately turns south, alongside a chalk pit. The way lies through a compact thicket of ash and elderberry trees, then along the right-hand side of a hedge.

Soon the way lies over a stile and down into a narrow side valley, taking you via a good bridleway down into Vessey Pasture Dale, the name given to the head of Court Dale. From here the valley heads east and becomes known as Back Dale, then Honey Dale ,before swinging to the south and taking the name of Court Dale.

St. Martin's Church at Wharram Percy has a rather cracked headstone fastened to the inside wall which bears the name of the Vessey family, while the farm up on the hill to the north-west is known as Vessey Pasture. However, from the bottom of Vessey Pasture Dale, a gate leads around a little knoll to the right and across to a hawthorn hedge halfway up the opposite hillside. This is Vessey Hill, and the way is steep but obvious, following, as it does, part of the Wolds Way.

Atop Vessey Hill the way levels out and turns left, passing a chalky pit full of farmyard rubbish. Beyond here a signpost points towards Cow Wold Barn, a few farm buildings surrounded by trees. Pass to the right of the barn and climb a stile to pick up a path through another hawthorn-smattered hillside. A good chalk track leads diagonally downhill to the western end of Thixendale village and so back to the start.

In all this walk as described is three miles long and can be completed in about an hour. To take the diversion to Wharram Percy will add a further two miles or so and will require another two hours if time is allowed to explore the medieval village.

Chapter Eighteen

Coxwold and Byland Abbey

This beautiful area lies in the north-west corner of the Howardian Hills, and purists would no doubt insist that it should have been excluded from a book about walking in East Yorkshire. True, it does lie almost on the very doorstep of the North York Moors, and, in fact, is the only walk in this book to be within the boundary of the National Park. However, I feel that geographically it has more in common with the other walks in the Howardian Hills than anything on 'the moors'. It cannot be denied that it is a fine area to explore, and for that reason alone I have included it here.

Historically the two villages which lie at either end of this walk are very interesting, although, as we start our walk at Coxwold, I shall describe that pleasant village first and come to Byland Abbey in due course. Minor roads radiate in all directions from the village, but perhaps suffice it say that the best approach is from either Easingwold five miles to the south or from Thirsk, a slightly greater distance to the north-west.

The wonderful octagonal tower of St. Michael's church dominates the Coxwold skyline, while stone houses line the roadsides. The wide cobbled verges are the remains of the long front gardens that each house once had to raise their livestock and grow what vegetables they could.

The church itself once had the famous author Laurence Sterne as its vicar. He was born in 1713, though some discrepancy has arisen as to the exact date of his death. In the churchyard there are two separate gravestones commemorating him, one stating that he died on 13 September 1768, while the other claims that the date was 18 March 1768. It is known, however, that this latter date is the correct one, but it cannot be determined how the other headstone came about.

Sterne's books are still widely read today, particularly

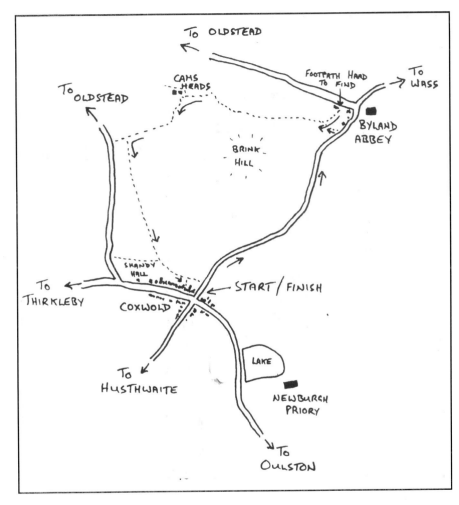

Wednesday and Sunday afternoons. The house, or at least part of it, is known to date as far back as the 14th century, and was always used as the priest's residence. Behind a wall panel is a hidden painting dating back to the very earliest days of the house, though this was not discovered until restoration work began on the house with a view to opening it to the public.

There is a good pub in the village, the Fauconberg Arms, which has much of Robert Thompson, 'The Mouseman of Kilburn's' work inside. Thompson was born in the nearby village of Kilburn in 1876, the son of the village joiner and carpenter, and, as was often the case, took to his father's trade on leaving school with little more than a knowledge of the three R's. Thompson is known throughout the world as the famous 'Mouseman' from the carvings of mice that he added to most of his ecclesiastical work. Examples of his work can be found throughout the country, though not all of his work was undertaken in churches. It is perhaps no surprise to find his mice in St. Michael's in Coxwold as well as in the Fauconberg Arms, merely two miles from his home.

Our walk can be started either from the Fauconberg Arms or from a public car park on the Byland Abbey road. Either way you must begin by walking the mile and a half along the road to Byland Abbey, a not too horrible

the one after which he named the house in which he lived in the village. Shandy Hall was named from *The Life and Opinions of Tristram Shandy, Gentleman,* perhaps his best-known work, though others included *The Sentimental Journey* and *Journey to Eliza.* Shandy Hall is often regarded as something of a literary shrine, and is open to the public during the summer months on proposition given the wide grass verges and the excellent views. From the pub head east for a hundred yards to a cross-roads and turn left. The public car park lies just beyond a petrol station on the right.

Continuing along the road on foot, take time to admire the work of John Hodgson, the schoolmaster in Kilburn. On the southern scarp of the North York Moors the famous White Horse is cut into the steep hillside. The idea was that of Thomas Taylor, a local man who was to become a London businessman. On a visit to the horse at Uffingham he immediately had a vision of a similar horse on Roulston Scar above his home village. Initially his idea was shunned by the locals, but eventually Hodgson decided to take up the challenge. After drawing up a plan, Hodgson supervised the construction by his pupils and 33 local men, finally seeing its completion on 4 November 1857. The White Horse measures a remarkable 314 feet in length and 228 in height. It is said that 20 people can stand on the eye of the horse, though that is discouraged due to the soft nature of the rock. Every few years the horse is whitened with limestone and chalk chips by volunteers, although on such a severe gradient the work is difficult in the extreme.

The horse is in full view throughout much of the walk along the road to Byland Abbey, though, as you climb

The ruins of Byland Abbey, nestling beneath the southern scarp of the North York Moors.

gently to a ridge that comes down from the flat-topped Brink Hill on the left, the old remains of Byland Abbey draw the eye away from the hillside.

This, the largest Cistercian church in England, was

founded in 1177 and is also reputed to have the largest nave in the country. The ruins are very interesting and are well worth a visit, though there is a charge as the site now belongs to English Heritage.

There is little else in the village of Byland Abbey, just a few stone farmhouses and cottages and the homely Abbey Inn. The hillsides to the north are cloaked in wonderfully coloured trees and are a delight to walk through if time permits. This hillside was the scene of the little known Battle of Byland in 1322. Edward II was resting at Byland Abbey after one of his frequent raids into Scotland when the advancing Scots army caught up with him. It will be remembered that this was just eight years after the massacre of Bannockburn where Edward

was defeated on his way to relieve the troops at Stirling. Some people, it would seem, just never learn. Suffering a grave defeat after being outflanked at Byland, Edward retreated to York to continue the conquest of Scotland from there. He was to be murdered five years later, and was succeeded by Edward III who began the Hundred Years War against France.

From Byland Abbey the Ordnance Survey map shows a public footpath heading south from the yard of College Farm. Taking the minor lane beside the Abbey Inn, this path starts just through the arch of an old gatehouse. By rights the way should lie through the farmyard and to the left of the buildings, but there is no evidence of this on the ground. The farm has a definite private feel to it, and it is likely that the right of access has not been asserted for some time.

If you do not feel up to an altercation with the farmer I would suggest retracing your steps along the road for 200 yards towards Coxwold. Just beyond a bend the road climbs a small rise and a public footpath sign on the right points across a field beside the right-hand boundary. This path isn't shown on the map, so it is possible that it is an agreed diversion to that shown going through the farm.

The way crosses pasture-land and passes to the north of Brink Hill. Following the path to Cam Heads, you find another public footpath heading south to a small deciduous copse. After passing the thicket turn right and follow the north side of a hedge towards a minor road near Fox Folly Farm.

Before reaching the road, however, a path branches off to the left and heads south across fields, eventually passing to the north of Shandy Hall and to the outskirts of Coxwold village. A public footpath can be found leading along the right-hand side of the Fauconberg Arms, or else you can continue eastwards to the minor road to Byland Abbey. This path brings you out at the road opposite the entrance to the public car park.

In all the walk is around four miles long and should take around three hours if time is given to explore the buildings of Coxwold and Byland Abbey. Whilst in the area it is also worthwhile heading east for half a mile from the cross-roads in Coxwold to Newburgh Priory. This Augustinian Friary was founded in 1145 and is reputedly the resting place of Oliver Cromwell. His body was brought here by his daughter, wife of the 2nd Viscount Fauconberg of Newburgh. The Priory is open on Wednesdays and Sundays throughout the summer months, and is well worth a visit.

A large lake is reached just before the Priory and ornithologists will find it worth a look. It is a regular breeding and over-wintering site for wildfowl.

Chapter Nineteen

Walking along the Hull Valley

Mention the Hull Valley to any local person, and you will inevitably get a blank stare. The area surrounding the River Hull is to all intents and purposes pretty flat, although this river, like all others, has carved its own course through these flat carr-lands, finding the lowest possible ground on its way to the Humber Estuary at Kingston upon Hull, and ultimately to the North Sea, gouging a very shallow valley en route. To the west of the river, the terrain rises in gentle folds and hidden hollows to the chalky hills of the Wolds chain, while to the east, and I must admit, it is barely perceptible, the terrain rises again to the Holderness Plain. This plain lies on average around 15 metres above sea level, while the Carrs of the Hull Valley struggle to reach five metres above sea level. And so I feel that I am justified in referring to the area taken by this walk as the middle Hull Valley.

The start of the walk is Hull Bridge just to the west of the village of Tickton, a small collection of houses just off the main road to the coast from Beverley, the busy A1035. At Hull Bridge cars can be left by the Anchor pub, and, if the walk is followed throughout, will be returned to in about seven hours. In total the length of the walk is 11½ miles, though it should be born in mind that it passes through the Tophill Low National Nature Reserve, and it is well worth spending a couple of hours exploring the ponds, reservoirs and marsh areas here. The seven hours stated allow for these diversions, though some visitors to the Reserve spend a full day there. Unless you are a member of the Hull Valley Wildlife Group, you will have to pay a small fee for entrance to the Reserve (£2.50 at present), though I am sure you will agree that this is well worth it, and indeed is good value for a full day's enjoyment. (Details of joining the Hull Valley Wildlife Group can be found at Tophill Low, and the address of the membership secretary is also given in the appendix to this book. Also note that the Reserve is closed to non-members on Mondays and Tuesdays every week.)

From the Anchor pub walk across the foot bridge which spans the River Hull and follow the road westwards for a hundred yards. A public bridleway heads north alongside Barmston Drain and should be followed, passing Riverside Cottages. After about half a mile the disused South Bullock Pumping Station is reached and, soon after, the drain ceases to run exactly parallel to the River Hull and turns towards the north-west. Continue along the eastern banks of the drain, passing a footbridge on the left which gives access to a track which leads to the large farm complex of Arram Grange and on to the village of Arram. Our way, however, stays beside the drain, rejoining the banks of the River Hull where a bridge crosses the Arram Beck.

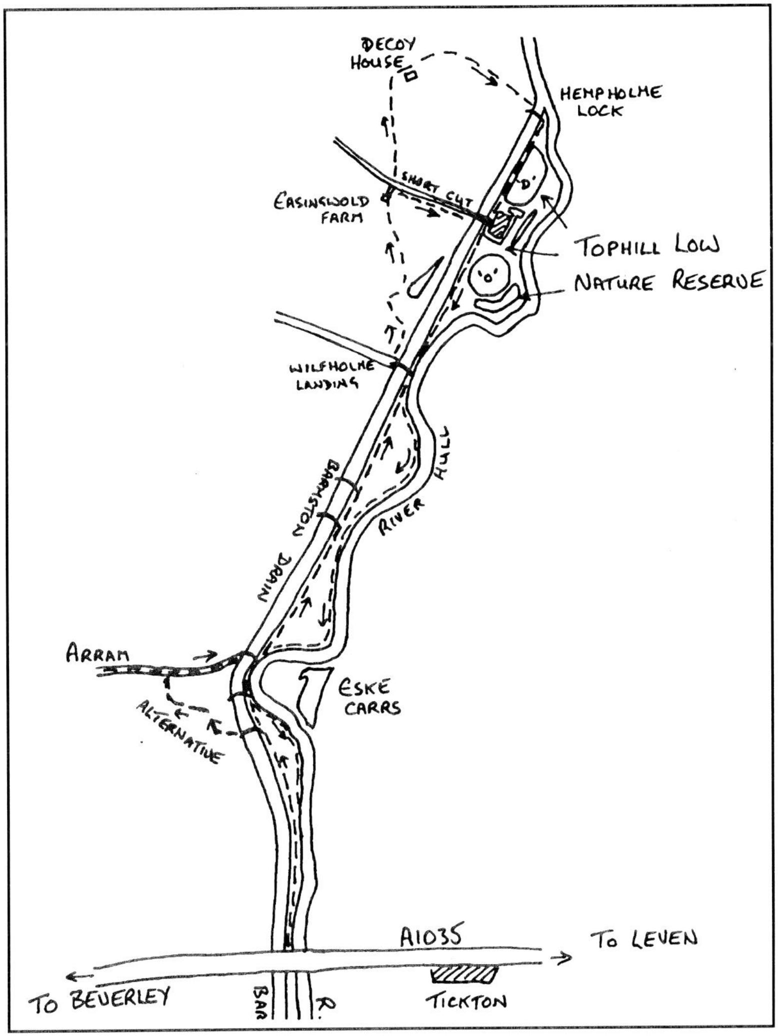

Again the river sweeps away to the east, forming the open fen land known as Pulfin and the High Eske Nature Reserves. These are important habitats for a number of bird species, though they do not offer much more than the Tophill Low Reserve.

Continuing along the eastern side of the drain, there is a path heading westwards for the village of Aike, reached by following the filled-in Aike Beck. However, there is nothing of interest to the walker in Aike, and you should continue along the drain across Aike Carrs to Wilfholme Bridge.

Pass Three Jolly Tars Farm by on the right and continue to a small car park at the pumping station at Wilfholme Landing. Crossing Watton Beck via a bridge, the path splits into two distinct public rights of way. Ignore the one along the River Hull to the right (you will come back that way after exploring Tophill Low) and pass through a gate into a muddy field full of ponies to come to the edge of the Watton Nature Reserve. Now the Barmston Drain should

DECOY HOUSE
HEMPHOLME LOCK
SHORT CUT
EASINGWOLD FARM
TOPHILL LOW NATURE RESERVE
WILFHOLME LANDING
BARMSTON DRAIN
RIVER HULL
ARRAM
ALTERNATIVE
ESKE CARRS
A1035
TO LEVEN
TO BEVERLEY
BAR
TICKTON

The visitor centre at the Tophill Low Nature Reserve. Arguably the finest Reserve in the East Riding.

The South Lagoon at Tophill Low. Just one of the many areas provided with hides.

be on your right. Here the public footpath leaves the drain side to head around the back of Easingwold Plantation, an area of open scrub.

A public hide gives fine views over two small lakes known as Watton Barrow Pits. These were formed when large amounts of clay were removed to strengthen and heighten the flood banks of the River Hull. Now they form an important habitat for a number of species of duck, including mallard, tufted duck, goldeneye, shelduck, smew and goosander, and the water margins are often alive with waders and the occasional cormorant in winter. It is very important that you remain quiet around these areas of the reserve, as all these birds 'spook' easily. It is worth carrying a pair of binoculars to ease viewing over these large expanses of water from the hide. Watton Nature Reserve is also botanically a very important site, hosting some very rare species of plant, some of which only frequent small areas of this region.

From the public hide, which is not part of the Tophill Low complex and is free for all to use, head north across rough ground towards Easingwold Farm. The access road for Tophill Low is gained just beyond the farm, and a public footpath sign near Whitedrain Bridge points alongside a field boundary behind a hedge. Follow this to turn north again alongside Decoy Drain. These fields are often full of thousands of geese and gulls in winter, and can be a spectacular sight.

If time is short, you can easily follow the road into the reserve, heading first for the main car park to pay for your day ticket, and thereby miss out the walk across to the Decoy fields to the north of the Reserve.

Heading north, the footpath emerges onto a track on which you should turn right towards Decoy Farm, passing it on the left. Soon the track swings around the northern edge of Decoy Wood before a path heads north towards a small drain. Head east alongside this drain to Hempholme Weir where Barmston Drain and the River Hull converge.

From Hempholme Weir you can enter the Tophill Low Nature Reserve, albeit by a back door. A track runs south-west beside a large D-shaped reservoir and eventually into a car parking area on the Reserve. Please do not look over the reservoir walls as this frightens the birds, some of which may be very rare indeed. Hides are provided for ticket holders and allow easy viewing for all. Day tickets should be purchased from a machine in the car park.

Alternatively, the public footpath runs along the outside of the Reserve boundary fence, beside the eastern side of Barmston Drain. You can follow this back to Wilfholme Bridge by simply heading south-west if you are not interested in entering the Reserve.

On the Reserve a Wildlife Centre near the car park should be visited for information on the area and what birds can be seen at the time of your visit. Many different species of ducks, geese, swans, waders, gulls and passerines [a collective term for thousands of tiny birds world-wide – it includes the sparrows, finches, tits, warblers and many more, the true definition being a perching bird] can be seen if you know where to look and what to look for, along with all manner of other birds, mammals, insects and flora. A warden, Mr. Peter Izzard, is usually on hand to offer advice and information.

To leave Tophill Low and head back to Hull Bridge, take the road out, passing the water treatment works. Turning left at the gate to the works, you reach a bridge which crosses over Barmston Drain and a public bridleway runs along the near, eastern side of this. Follow this south, back to Wilfholme Landing.

From Wilfholme Landing you can either retrace your steps alongside Barmston Drain, or, for views across the River Hull, which has so far been hidden by a flood bank, a footpath runs across the top of the flood bank. The way is less direct than the drain, but is pleasant throughout.

Chapter Twenty

Ampleforth and Yearsley Moor

A rough stretch of land, forestry interspersed with arable fields and deep valleys, lies to the east of the A19 road near Easingwold. This is the wonderful range known as the Howardian Hills. In the south-east of the range lies Castle Howard and the deep valley of the Derwent, a country explored in Chapter Sixteen of this book, whilst to the north-west, almost where the Howardian Hills begin to merge with the Oolitic limestone hills of Hambleton, we find the villages of Coxwold and Byland Abbey, previously discovered on foot in Chapter Eighteen. Sandwiched in between these areas the terrain is predominantly forested, with open acres of gorse and heather scrub filling in the gaps between the plantations. This is Yearsley Moor, the area to which this chapter is devoted. I make no apologies for including this walk in this book, for this really is delightful walking country, and, although well outside the Wolds chain of hills, this area doesn't really fit very well into any other geographical region.

A little used B road, the B1363, runs north from Sutton-on-the-Forest to Osbaldkirk on the Malton to Helmsley road, and at a small village called Brandsby a lane climbs up a broad ridge to the hamlet of Yearsley. The houses are centred around a cross-roads, and here you should go straight ahead, heading north-west. Ignore a minor lane on the left which leads to Oulston and Coxwold, and, continuing, a forestry track leaves the road on the right just 200 yards beyond this junction. Turn onto this track, signposted as 'Windygate'

and park on the verge beside a fenced-off track on the left.

This whole area was bought by the Forestry Commission back in the early 1920s. During the First World War much timber had had to be imported into Britain for essential rebuilding work, and this had put an unbearable strain on the available shipping during the already difficult war years. Following the war, in 1919, the government established the Forestry Commission with the overall plan of making the whole country self-supporting in timber in the event of any future emergency of at least three-years' duration. Properties of a suitably low commercial value, such as high-level moorland and grassland, which is of little economic use, were purchased and planted with quick-growing softwoods. Unfortunately these were often of non-native conifers such as Sitka

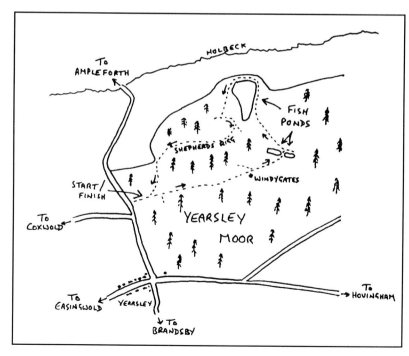

spruce from North America, Norway Spruce and Japanese Larch. The initial plan was to plant up 1,777,000 acres throughout England, Scotland and Wales. But just as planting got underway, Parliament began a series of cuts in the forestry budget, and only a small percentage of this area saw the first plantations taking shape. All of this, of course, was much too late for the next national emergency. The start of the Second World War saw the country in little better shape than had the First, but after 1945 the timber plan really began in earnest and the Commission took on the task of planting 3,000,000 new acres, and re-planting 2,000,000 acres of old woodland.

The forests of Yearsley Moor belong to the period of the very early plantings of the Forestry Commission. Work began in 1928 with planting of small blocks of around 400 acres, and some of these areas can still be seen today, although by far the majority of the existing trees in the forest belong to the post-1945 era of planting. This regeneration continues to this day.

Not so long ago it was felt by many that the Forestry Commission had desecrated huge areas of wild land, and that by importing alien species of tree, which grow faster than our own species, had limited the natural habitats of many of our native woodland animals. Even the Commission admit that much of their early work followed incredibly single-minded planting techniques,

Dusk at the lower Fishpond, Yearsley Moor.

and can only be described as bad forestry management. Now, the Forestry Commission takes great pains to plant up areas of deciduous trees such as aspen, birch and rowan to encourage wildlife, and often these areas are linked together through the forests with corridors of scrub along which animals and birds can pass.

Many still find it hard to forget the past malpractice of the Forestry Commission, and will not honestly credit that the Commission is now a leading light in many aspects of conservation. The Forestry Commission these days actively encourages people to explore their forests, and some areas even have visitor centres, display boards and guided tours.

Personally, I find these forests to be a hive of wild activity, and if you know where to look you can often seen siskins, goldcrests or crossbills picking seeds from the pine cones in the tree tops, or a secretive roe deer bobbing away through the ground cover. As you follow this short walk through the forest keep a look out for the wild creatures who live their lives here.

Yearsley Moor is a wonderful place to explore, although for the visitor there are no such amenities as can be found in Dalby Forest to the east, or Cleveland Forest near Silton to the north.

From the parking place on the track to Windygates, ignore all other tracks which leave the main one and walk north-eastwards along this main track. Soon the trees give way on the left to a harvested area across which the southern edge of the North York Moors National Park can be seen. These Tabular Hills rise above the village of Ampleforth, to the east of which lies the famous College to which some of the land crossed later in the walk belongs. Above the village to the north lies one of the finest enclosure-type earthworks of the Iron Age in the area. The Studford Ring is 54 yards in diameter, with a rampart 24-foot wide. Excavations on the site have revealed nothing at all, although similar, smaller rings have yielded Iron Age pottery. Archaeologists believe the Studfold, as it is also known, to be the ring of a horse compound which increased in importance during that period.

Beyond this view-point the track bends slightly to the right and brings you to the cottage and out-buildings that make up Windygates, surely one of the most lovely places on Earth to live. From Windygates the way continues, still ignoring all side tracks, as ours continues down into the area of forest known as The Wilderness. Soon a track cuts across ours at right-angles, and the way on lies down a muddy path between clumps of over-grown rhododendrons and down to the banks of a small fish pond. Mallards are usually in evidence here, and, if you look closely, there is always the chance that reed buntings may be among the rushes and reed mace along the western shore.

The path actually crosses an embankment which, it will soon become clear, is in effect a dam, below which lies a second pond, initially hidden among the trees. Once across the dam a good track crosses our path at a T junction. Turn left here and follow the main path alongside the lower of the two ponds.

Wonderful birch trees of great age flourish alongside the track and occasional clumps of heather and bilberry grow in the patches of light that aren't over-shadowed by the old rhododendrons.

Soon the two small ponds are left behind, and, as the way drops downhill slightly, a much larger fish pond looms out of the trees and shrubs. Although the public footpath here lies some way above the pond, a path has been trodden by thousands of pupils from Ampleforth College who own this part of the valley, alongside the shore, and many will want to take to this path. Small jetties provide ideal picnic sites for those who have come prepared, and this surely is the best place for this on the entire walk. Once you've rested awhile by the pond, continue around its perimeter, crossing an earthen dam to a point where a small footbridge leads across a fast-flowing culvert.

From now on you must leave the well-signposted public footpaths and find a way along the many unmarked forest rides. A muddy path leaves the dam at its north-western end and heads uphill back into the thick of the forest. Soon a wider track is reached, and at a junction you should turn left. This leads initially downhill to bring you out at a contouring track with much open scrub on the left. The way here is obvious, and soon the main track turns sharply right to begin a steady climb uphill. To the left runs a stream amid old oak tree stumps and birch thicket. This stream follows the gully of Elder Slack, and you should follow this main track uphill throughout. It edges away from Elder Slack to swing around the ridge known as Shepherd's Rigg, perhaps a reference to the days before the trees came, although I once tried to follow a more direct route up right beside the stream. The way soon became entangled with fallen trees and much bramble, and I had to turn around and fight my way back through the undergrowth to the main track.

Other paths head off into the trees at intervals, but the main track is obvious throughout and should be kept underfoot. It leads, within half a mile, back to the car park atop Newton Hill where this walk started, barely three miles and an hour previously – though, I would recommend carrying a picnic and spending half a day exploring the forest.

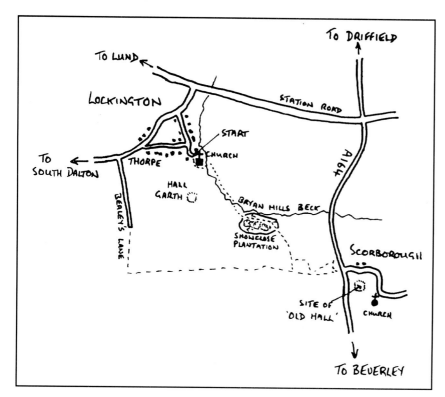

Chapter Twenty One

Lockington and Scorborough

The quaint village houses and stately trees of Lockington grace both banks of the gurgling Bryan Mills Beck which flows through the centre of the village. Lockington is a peaceful place, seemingly made up of farms set in a timeless age, and delightful cottages lining the quiet streets. It lies just over a mile west of the busy A164, about mid-way between Leconfield and Hutton Cranswick where a minor lane, known as Station Road, leads across Cottage Pasture to the village. The Rockingham Arms is the central point of village life, and,

although our route does not actually pass its pumps, it is only a short detour to do so. The village itself is on the site of an Anglo-Saxon settlement which made use of the water from the beck.

You should start at St. Mary's church to the south of the village centre. A minor road, known as Church Lane, passes between high-walled gardens and avenues of trees to a car park beside the Rectory. St. Mary's dates back to Norman times and has a good example of a 14th-century brick tower. Within the church you will find a fine display of heraldry in the Estoft Chapel.

The churchyard is also of some importance, though for a very different reason. Here we are reminded that it is a sanctuary for the living as well as for the dead. Ten years ago, under the initiative of Dr. John Habgood, at that time Archbishop of York, the Diocese of York and the Yorkshire Wildlife Trust got together to discuss the relative merits of stimulating local interest in the management of churchyards in ways that would benefit the native flora and fauna that make these places their home. The Yorkshire Living Churchyards Project was founded as a joint venture, and now over 150 churchyards have had management plans drawn up with a view geared towards wildlife conservation. St. Mary's of Lockington is one such site, and provides a valuable habitat for flowers, birds, insects and small mammals that would otherwise struggle to survive.

The scheme also has the positive side of encouraging local rural communities to care more for the wildlife that

can be found in their villages. It is hoped that this management initiative in the churchyard has extended beyond the boundary of the church grounds to take in other parts of the village. This is certainly the case in Lockington, as every garden appears to have bird tables and nut bags hung from trees. On my last visit during one of the coldest spells of the year, the whole village was a hive of flitting birds enjoying the wealth of food put out for them by the village residents.

Start at the church car park. (Please note that this is not a public car park and is for the use of church goers only, though on quiet days there seems to be no objection to the odd car or two parking there. If in doubt park in the village and walk down the road to the church.) A public footpath sign points through the churchyard and passes the western entrance before heading east through an avenue of trees to cross a narrow foot-bridge over Bryan Mills Beck. Straight ahead lies Carriage Drive, though our way climbs a stile to the right and follows the eastern, true left bank of the beck.

Across the field to the right lies Hall Garth Farm, built on the site of an old wooden castle. Typical features of this treed and moated site can still be seen, although this must be from a distance as the way over to the farm is private. It once belonged to the Constable family, though the present building itself dates as far back as 1685. Soon the path leaves the side of the beck and crosses a narrow plank of a bridge with a stile at either end. A broad pasture is crossed and posts lead the way through a boggy section, replete with hard rushes.

So far the route has followed part of the Minster Way, a 50-mile walk that links the two magnificent Minsters at York and Beverley through some of the best scenery in the Wolds. The way heads for the eastern corner of the pasture at a gate leading into Snowclose Plantation. The Ordnance Survey map show the wood just to the south of the path, but, since the map was printed, other trees, both coniferous and deciduous, have also been planted to the north, albeit in a very narrow belt as far as the banks of the Bryan Mills Beck. The way is obvious as chicken-wire fencing runs along both sides of the track, effectively keeping you from wandering off into the woods.

Once through Snowclose Plantation, the path heads off in a south-east direction, straight across the middle of an arable field. It is, however, easy to follow, as the way is walked often and an eroded path cuts through the crops. By now the steeple of Scorborough church can be seen piercing the sky above the tall trees that grow around the village. This is to be our turn-around point on this walk.

Once you are across the field, another plank-bridge

A crisp winter's day by the Bryan Mills Beck, with Lockington Church in the background.

gives access to more arable land, and the path leads off around the right-hand perimeter of the next field. Just beyond a large ash tree which grows at the field's edge a public footpath sign points at right angles across the middle of the field to the left. Our way takes this path, but for those of you who are ready for returning to Lockington without taking in Scorborough, it is possible to ignore this sign and continue for a further 200 yards along the edge of the field to another sign. The longer way comes back to this point shortly, and I shall describe the route from here presently.

Heading across the middle of the field, you keep to the route which still follows the Minster Way signs, first to the right upon reaching the far side, then alongside a hedge to a corner. A public footpath makes for Lakes Farm just off the A164, and the drive can be followed out to that busy road.

Immediately opposite, Scorborough Lane twists in narrow curves around an open pasture to the south, while pleasant cottages line the northern side. The lane soon leads to Scorborough Church. The original church was of Norman design, though only the font and a carved figure of a priest remain from the original building. This church was rebuilt in 1859 by J. L. Pearson.

The open pasture land around which Scorborough Lane curves is the site of the old Scorborough Hall, shown on an old estate map of 1616 as 'Mr. Hothams House'. It was Sir John Hotham, Governor of Hull, who in 1642 closed the gates to King Charles I. On 23 April Charles rode with 300 gentlemen from Beverley to Hull with the intention of dining with the Governor. Upon arrival, Sir John Hotham stated from the battlements of the town walls that he had been ordered not to admit the King. This was to give Hull the dubious honour of being the first town in the country to rebel against the Crown. Sir John Hotham, however, was to be tried for high treason, and he was beheaded on Tower Hill.

The Hothams had lived at Scorborough from the mid-13th century, and became one of the most influential landed families in the three Ridings. The Hall was destroyed by fire in 1705-6 and was not rebuilt, though the Hothams eventually went on to establish their family seat at South Dalton.

To return to Lockington you must again cross the busy A164 and take the driveway back up to Lakes Farm. From the Minster Way signpost beyond the farm buildings, a public bridleway sign points across a field to the sign mentioned earlier as being the point of return for those wishing to miss out a visit to Scorborough Church. After you have crossed another field heading westwards, a field boundary is soon reached beside a small overgrown pond, and the track is obvious as it follows hawthorn hedgerows westwards around the fields to the north of Bealey's Plantation.

A small copse of trees and scrub on the right is reached before passing through a gateway, ignoring a stile taken by a public footpath to the right, and another public footpath sign which heads off to the south towards Leconfield.

Soon a wide rutted track which runs north to south is gained. Here you should turn right and follow this track, known as Bealey's Lane, northwards. The lane soon becomes more solid underfoot as tarmac takes the place of muddy scrapes, and the way continues back to Lockington.

A minor road is reached at the western edge of the village, known as Thorpe, and a right turn, followed by another right, leads back to the church after a pleasant three-hour walk.

Chapter Twenty Two

Staxton Wold

To the north of Great Driffield the general trend of the Wolds turns from a north-south direction to an east-west one, and the steep scarp that forms the western edge of these chalky hills now falls away to the Carrs to the north. These carrs once held the great glacial lake that filled the Vale of Pickering, and our walk along the top of the scarp overlooks this plain to the moorland ridges of the North York Moors National Park.

Before we can gain this wonderful view-point, we must first climb onto the

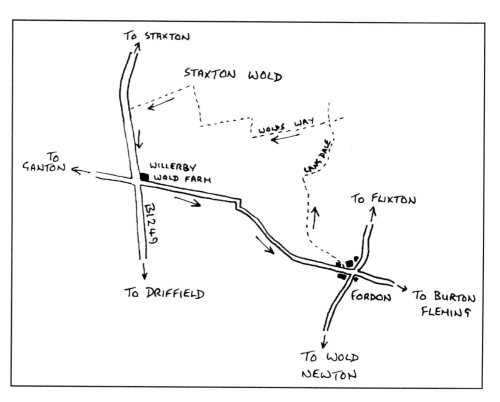

hills of these northern Wolds. One of the very best places to start a walk in this region is the tiny hamlet of Fordon, tucked away in a gentle fold of the hills, a real backwater in this already quiet area.

Heading north along the B1249 from Driffield, the road passes through Langtoft, goes dead ahead at the Octon Cross Roads, now a roundabout, and continues to the village of Foxholes. Barely half a mile north of Foxholes a minor lane, known locally as the North Cotes Road, heads east along a high arable land of open fields. Soon this lane comes to a T-junction, and, while the road to the right heads south for the pleasant village of Wold Newton, you should turn left and head downhill to Fordon, passing an Ordnance Survey triangulation pillar

by the side of the road along the way.

Fordon lies at the confluence of West Dale and North Dale, though four roads also meet there. As you come to the cross-roads, just beyond a tiny chapel that lies among the old yew trees to the left, the village itself huddles down in the valley below the embankment upon which the chapel rests. The best place to park is to the right of the cross-roads on a wide grass verge, taking care not to block the gateway into the adjoining fields.

From the junction head west along the road below the chapel, passing the few farms that make up the village. At the very last farm on the right, Low Fordon, a public telephone box marks the start of the walk proper, and a crooked sign points alongside the farm buildings. Head

The start of the walk on to Staxton Wold: Low Fordon Farm.

Typical Wolds scenery across North Dale.

down this track and through a gate which is hard to miss, thanks to the large car number plate bearing the word 'FOOTPATH' in big letters across the top spell.

Closing the gate behind you, head into North Dale, a typical example of the wonderful scenery that can be found in these parts of the Wolds. Stunted hawthorns dot the hillsides, and sturdy ash trees grow in the meadows of the valley bottoms. To the left of this path lies a good blackthorn or sloe hedge. This is a wild form of the common garden tree, the ornamental cherry, though, like all members of the *Prunus* genus, it flowers copiously in the wild. This delightful thicket-forming tree, *Prunus spinosa,* is often used by country folk to make a deliciously fruity home-made wine, known as sloe gin.

The way is not all that obvious at first, a problem that seems to be caused mainly by lack of use and the fact that further up the dale the public footpath ends abruptly in the middle of nowhere. Beyond the hedge of blackthorn and young ash a stile leads out into a more open meadow, and a sign tacked to a post points along the right-hand side of a fence. A broken stile leads into the next fields as the dale curves around to the right, but the fence here is also broken, so crossing is an easy matter.

The hillside to the right is cloaked with gorse, the beautiful yellow furze of the legume family of plants. Its pea-like flowers brighten any wild corner of the Wolds from March until May, though it is known that certain parts of the plant are poisonous, containing the alkaloid cytisin. The rough ground beneath these gorse bushes provides an excellent warren for rabbits, and some small farmland birds such as the yellowhammer, corn bunting, whinchat and finches can often be seen singing from a thorny perch.

I have walked along this dale on perhaps half a dozen or more occasions, and on four of those have been lucky enough to seen a kestrel hunting along the gorse thickets. While rabbits are far too large a prey for the kestrel, smaller mammals such as voles, mice and shrews form a good part of their diet, so there must be a plentiful supply hereabouts.

Soon the path, which by now is running along the open bottom of the dale, passes through a narrow belt of trees and continues to a point where the pasture-land of the valleys has been tilled to form arable fields. A gate lies to the left, but the way does not pass through it. Instead, the path heads right towards the corner of a hawthorn copse. A stile can be seen crossing an electric fence and the path borders the edge of the field with the fence to the right. Within a quarter of a mile a gateway leads to a group of sheep folds at the confluence of Cotton Dale and Lang Dale. Here the public right of way officially ends, on the map at least, though a good path does lead up Lang Dale to the right to join the Wolds Way atop Flixton Wold. As I have said, this is private property, though I have seen other walkers using this path, and on two occasions when I have passed this way myself have come across the farmer attending to his sheep and have not been apprehended by him. The continuation of this walk heads up Lang Dale, but you should bear this access problem in mind.

Go through a gate, usually tied up with string, so remember to re-fasten it, and walk up the grassy valley of Lang Dale. A sheep track leads the way, though, as the vegetation is close-cropped turf, there is no need to stick to this.

Soon an ablation valley [the term for a valley formed by the course of a glacier or water] comes in from the right, heavily cloaked with hawthorns and gorse, and just beyond, in the valley bottom, a gate leads into the next field. Just 200 yards beyond the gate, the Wolds Way crosses over at right angles. From now onwards you are again following public rights of way.

Turn left and follow the Wolds Way over the head of a number of minor valley which fall away to the south into Cotton Dale. Stiles give access from one field to the next and the going is easy. This is the plateau-land of

Staxton Wold. Soon the way leads first right for a couple of hundred yards, then back left. A stile climbs a fence at the point where the Wolds Way descends steeply into the head of Cotton Dale amid much scrub, though a good track is soon reached climbing out of the valley.

Turn right on this part-tarmac lane and climb steadily up to where the dale merges with the flatlands of the top of the Wold. A farm on the left is passed before the imposing buildings, radio masts and dishes of RAF Staxton Wold are reached. This is one of the MOD's early warning stations and in the interests of national security it is advisable not to take photographs nearby.

The station opened on 1 April 1939 and immediately began monitoring the various flight positions of the Luftwaffe. The safety of the base was always ensured, until December 1942 when the RAF very nearly scored something of an own goal. A Halifax bomber on an operational flight struggled back to Britain with its fuselage on fire, and passing over Staxton Wold was forced to dump a load of incendiary bombs and a 1,000-lb bomb onto a nearby field. That night was the only occasion that the base came close to being bombed itself.

The way now is along the tarmac approach road for RAF Staxton Wold, and some people will find this part of the walk as interesting as any other. Soon, however, a left turn along the road leaves the base behind, and a long straight section of road leads out to the B1249 at Grange Farm.

A rather dangerous part of the walk follows as you turn left along the busy road and head south for just under a mile to a cross-roads at Willerby Wold Farm. Here a set of white gates is fixed to block the road, but they are invariably left open, and you should turn left again onto the minor lane which passes the farm.

A further two and a half miles of road walking, albeit along a very quiet section, then leads back to Fordon across the top of Prior Moor, after six and a half miles of walking in around three hours.

Chapter Twenty Three

Sledmere and Kirby Grindalythe

The pleasant little village of Sledmere stands at the junction of a number of roads criss-crossing this part of the Wolds. The B1251, B1252 and B1253 all converge here, as do three minor roads, all meeting within the environs of Sledmere House, the large manor house of the Sykes family which dominates the village.

During the early part of its life, the original Sledmere House saw few regular occupiers, being nothing much greater than a base from which to hunt the surrounding district. This was back in medieval times when the Wolds were among the wildest areas of the country. That the area was primitive is evident in that it is known that well into the 17th century wolves still preyed upon the livestock of the villages of the district.

Towards the middle of the 17th century the property was purchased by Mark Kirkby, a descendant of Sir Robert Kirkby of Cottingham, who at the time owned vast estates in Holderness. Mark Kirkby (or Kirby) became the first to make a real home of the then Tudor manor house which stood in the village. Since that day there has been an unbroken line of ownership of Sledmere House between the Kirkby family and their heirs the Sykes. Mark Kirkby's daughter, Mary, married Richard Sykes of Hull in 1703. Her older brother, also called Mark, later to become High Sheriff of Yorkshire in 1737, inherited Sledmere House from his father in 1718, and used it as his residence until he died in 1748. As Mark was childless, Sledmere, along with the many other estates which belonged to the family, passed on via his sister Mary Sykes. The Sykes also came from a long family line, traceable as far back as Richard Sykes-Dyke of Cumberland, born around 1450.

Soon after the estates had passed to the Sykes family, the then heir, another Richard Sykes, born in 1706, laid plans to alter the house, and on 'June 17th, 1751 – Laid the first stone of the new house at Sledmere'.

The old house was totally demolished, and today nothing can be found of its existence, other than some of the original brickwork in the cellar. These alterations, which included building a new church, form the basic architectural shape that we see today. Other additions came through the years, most notably a 2,000-acre park

planted with plans drawn up by 'Capability' Brown, and the outer shell of the house changed by Sir Christopher Sykes in the 1780s to Nottinghamshire stone. During this time the aspect of the house was also altered so that the main front was turned to face south. Although other, smaller changes were made, the basic structure of the house remained in the style of Sir Christopher Sykes until 1911.

On 23 May 1911, a fire broke out in the kitchen of Sledmere House. An old beam which protruded into the chimney of the kitchen began to smoulder, and soon spread upwards into the roof of the house. Incredibly, all the contents of the house were salvaged, mainly due to the remoteness of the initial blaze. Even banisters and doors were removed, along with the contents of the library, while the fire continued to rage, eventually dying out after 18 hours. All that remained once the smouldering embers had died down were the four outer walls, the dairy and the laundry.

Restoration of the main residence began in 1912 and continued until 1917, each room being carefully worked on to re-create some of the 18th-century splendour of the house. Work in other rooms and outbuildings continued throughout most of the First World War, eventually being completed in 1926 under the ownership of the late Sir Richard Sykes. Today it encompasses all the character of a Georgian house, whilst remaining essentially Edwardian. The house is open to visitors during the summer months from April until the end of September, except on Saturdays and Mondays.

Perhaps best known of all the Sykes family are Sir Christopher and his son Sir Tatton, the fourth baronet. Sir Christopher reclaimed thousands of acres of wild land throughout the Wolds, turning them over to agriculture, and leaving us with the excellent farm land that we enjoy in the region today. Sir Tatton, though also respected throughout England as an agriculturalist, became famous throughout Yorkshire for his amazing feats of stamina. 'Old Tat' or 'Old Tatters', as he was affectionately known locally, regularly walked to livestock markets in Lincolnshire to buy sheep, and then drove them home himself. As a well-known jockey, he is credited with riding from Yorkshire to Aberdeen to jockey in a race for Lord Huntley, which he won, and then back to Doncaster in time for the St. Leger, which he always attended. A truly amazing feat, covering 740 miles in just five days!

Another Sir Tatton, his son, should be remembered for his work in restoring many of the old churches of our region and in building new ones.

Walking through Sledmere, you cannot help but be impressed by the well-preserved monuments that adorn the village. The most notable in the immediate environment is the Eleanor Cross, built in 1895 by Temple Moore for Sir Tatton Sykes the fifth baronet. Eleanor of Castile, the wife of Edward I, died in 1290 in Nottinghamshire, and these crosses were subsequently erected to

Eleanor Cross at Sledmere.

commemorate the resting places of her body on the way to London for burial. Charing Cross marks the end of this journey. The Eleanor Cross at Sledmere now stands as a memorial to those who fell during the First World War.

Just east of the Eleanor Cross, at the junction of the minor road to Kirby Grindalythe, stands the Waggoners' Memorial. This squat little monument commemorates the services of the Waggoners' Reserve, a company of over a thousand men of the Wolds farms who served in the First World War. It is this minor road from Kirby Grindalythe upon which we shall return after our walk around Thirkleby Wold to the north of the village.

Leaving the car at a car park beside the junction of the B1251 to Fimber and the B1253 to Duggleby, you should head east, passing the Eleanor Cross and the Waggoners' Memorial. The main house stands to the south behind a high wall and hedge, though it is evident that the other buildings in the village are part of the same estate.

Soon the village well is reached, built as you would expect as a memorial. The inscription reads:

'This Edifice was erected by Sir Tatton Sykes, Baronet, to the memory of his father, Sir Christopher Sykes, Baronet, who by assiduity and perseverance in building and planting and inclosing on the Yorkshire Wolds, in the short space of thirty years, set such an example to other owners of land, as has caused what once was a bleak and barren tract of country to become now one of the most productive and best cultivated districts in the County of York. A.D. 1840'

There is yet another well-known monument, standing atop Garton Hill on the road to Driffield, the B1252, built as a memorial to Sir Tatton Sykes, 4th Baronet, by his friends and neighbours in 1865. Although our route does not pass by its imposing needle-like structure, it is a familiar sight throughout this part of the Wolds, piercing the sky as it does to a height of over 100 feet.

Our route turns off the main road through the village, after passing the Triton Inn on the right. To the left the B1253 heads east towards Bridlington via the Octon Cross Roads, and you should follow this uphill until beyond the edge of the village.

At a small sports field on the left, a public footpath sign heads across the mouth of a football pitch goal towards the green silage tower of Croome House. Following this soon brings you to a good driveway which leaves the farm and heads back east for 200 yards until another path can be picked up heading north for the minor road through Croome Dale at Croome Farm.

Here you should turn right and follow the lane until a tarmac track leaves the road and climbs steadily uphill to the north towards the farm buildings at Thirkleby Wold. This climbs gradually to an Ordnance Survey triangulation pillar just beyond the farm buildings, before descending between hedges forming a green lane, to a public bridleway which heads west from the village of West Lutton. For those wishing to slake their thirst, there is a hostelry in West Lutton, the Three Tuns, but it should be noted that it is slightly off route. To reach the pub turn right onto the public bridleway and follow it easily into the village.

After a pint or two return along the bridleway from Sheepwalk Lane and continue past the junction from Thirkleby Wold, along the valley bottom. An obvious path follows the line of the beck, known as the Gypsey Race, which drains the fields of Kirby Grindalythe and Duggleby to the west. The way passes the vague re-entrant [a shallow valley or gully] known as Dollyth Howe shortly before entering the village of Kirby Grindalythe, a sleepy, quiet little place, via a field full of ponies and a gate leading to a car turning area beside a group of cottages. Follow the drive out to the right and alongside the beck

The tiny village of Kirby Grindalythe

to come to a junction of narrow roads. Turning left along the lane, signposted as to Sledmere, the way is easy and relatively free from traffic, although starting with a sharp ascent up Cromwell Hill.

The way eases, and a gentle rise leads to a narrow belt of beech and sycamore trees at the top of the hill. Crook Plantation lies to the right while Kirby Plantation lies to the left. Beyond, the lane descends to the wooded valley Hog Walk past a weed-filled pond on the right. The climb out of the Hog Walk still heading south along the lane is at first steep, but soon eases as it gains the top

of a long chalky ridge at the eastern nab of Towthorpe Wold. A small plantation of young beech saplings on the left of this, Kirby Lane is reached just prior to dropping down to the outskirts of Sledmere at the Waggoners' Memorial. All along this last section the way gives fine views over Sledmere House and Park to the south.

In all, this peaceful little walk is around eight miles long if the diversion into West Lutton is taken, and should take around three hours to complete, depending on how much time is spent drinking in the Three Tuns at the mid-way point, and in the Triton Inn upon finishing.

Chapter Twenty Four

The Driffield Canal

Great Driffield, often called the Capital of the Wolds, lies within the head-waters of the River Hull – one of the most important rivers of the East Riding. From an administrative point of view Driffield was included in the Bainton Beacon division of the old wapentake boundary of Harthill, a boundary which encompasses all of the land to the south, as far as what was then known as Hullshire, and as far west as the Derwent. Wapentakes were devised in the 12th century to replace the old 'hundreds' that were set out in Domesday Book. The four divisions of the Harthill wapentake were each responsible for the maintenance of a beacon within their own boundary, these divisions being made under Elizabeth I four centuries later.

Today near Great Driffield we find sparkling trout streams flowing from the inner curve of the higher Wolds where they bend towards the coast at Flamborough, and on, gurgling through the town to form the River Hull, while alongside, the man-made canal which once took barges down to the deeper waters of the river beyond Frodingham Beck and on to Beverley and Hull, stands quiet now, home only to ducks in places where house-boats once moored.

The canal opened in 1767 and was used to transport grain and other agricultural produce down river, the keels bringing back coal, building timber and fertilisers on their return journey. Throughout the country canals at this time were recognised as the chief means of commercial transportation, the only other alternative being by cart. Navigable waterways were constructed everywhere with a view to linking the major towns and cities of the country by water. Prior to the opening of the Driffield Navigation

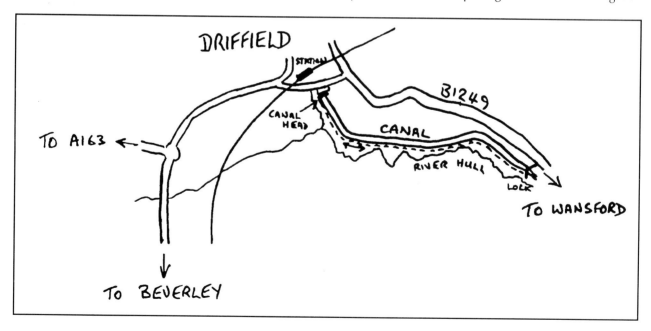

Canal the region already had four others, namely the Derwent Navigation, the Ouse Navigation, the newly deepened Beverley Beck and the improved Patrington Haven. Indeed the East Riding had made use of three navigable waterways as far back as the medieval period, serving the towns of Beverley, Hedon and Patrington. So it can be seen that the idea of a canal was certainly not a new one to the local people, and indeed many Driffield people considered the building of a canal to be essential to the further development of the Town. In 1762 William Porter, a Driffield businessman trading as a corn merchant and the landlord of what is now known as the Bell Inn, wrote: 'If a canal could be made from here to Hull, Driffield would soon emerge as one of the best market towns in the East Riding.' He was correct, and, largely through his instigation, the building of the canal began. By the mid-19th century Great Driffield had grown to become the most important grain market in the county, exporting well over 100,000 quarters of corn a year. All of this travelled down to the River Hull via the canal, a large part of it then continuing westwards up the River Humber and onto the network of canals which served the West Riding. By the year 1800 a total of 27 ships traded regularly along this route from Driffield. Other industries apart from agriculture grew up and benefited from the building of the canal, with paper mills, a whiting factory and other warehouses springing

Canal Head at Driffield.

91

up at the canal head and flourishing. Many of these buildings still stand today, though a good few of them now provide up-market residences rather than being used commercially.

With the coming of the railway through Driffield from Hull to the coast at Bridlington in 1846, a steady decline began in the commercial usage of the canal. Things worsened when the railway line was extended to Scarborough the following year, and by the turn of the century the canal had become almost obsolete and began to fall into disrepair.

Today, although some sections of the canal-sides have very good public footpath networks, quite infuriatingly, they often don't link up, and the walker must piece them together as best as he can, using roads to rejoin the canal further on. Fortunately, there are some good sections to walk, most notably the stretch from the Canal Head in Driffield which we shall follow here, and a walk from Wansford to Brigham near North Frodingham.

Our walk starts to the south of the railway station, which provides a good means of transport for those without their own, at a large car park beside some of the old mills on the canal banks.

Mallards, or 'wild duck' as they used to be known, and tufted duck join here with the odd-looking Muscovy or Chinese duck to collect bread thrown by the many visitors who come here for this purpose, while moorhens and coot bob along, largely minding their own business.

The Blue bell Inn near the Canal Head in Great Driffield

These latter two birds are very common members of the rail family [of the order *Rallidae* which includes the corncrakes and water rail] and can usually be seen anywhere where there is water. They are both predominantly dark-coloured, the coot being totally black except for a white bill and frontal shield (an obvious patch above the bill), and the moorhen having black undersides with a dark brown back. The moorhen has a red frontal shield and bill, with just a flick of yellow at its tip. It is also noticeably smaller than the coot.

Mute swans are also usually in evidence, gracefully plying the water with their dowdy-looking cygnets, and the little grebe can sometimes be seen here in small numbers. This diving bird is by far the smallest of the various members of the grebe family, appearing to the unknowing to be a fledgling of a duck. It is generally dark brown, but has a striking russet neck and a yellow spot behind its bill. In winter the colours generally fade, although this is not always the case if the weather remains mild. I always find it to be a wonderfully endearing little thing. On my last visit to the Canal Head there were six of them together, or at least paired off and sharing the same stretch of water. As I watched they each in turn had a go at bawling at me with their loud 'whit-whit' song, obviously an attempt at an alarm call to frighten me away, so I moved on and left them to it in peace. The little grebe is the only member of that family which fequents freshwater and estuaries exclusively. All of the others, comprising four other species in Britain (great crested, red-necked, Slavonian and black-necked grebes), can also be seen around coastal waters as well as inland.

And so, after drinking in the atmosphere of the Blue Bell Inn and the old warehouses around the Canal Head, and feeding the ducks with your packed lunch, you can start on your walk. In all, we shall follow the southern banks of the canal for barely a little over a mile to a point where a bridge gives access to the B1249 road from Driffield to Wansford at a lock. To continue further would involve a good deal of road walking before we could again join the canal, and I would not recommend that to anyone. Besides, your walk from the Canal Head will undoubtedly involve a short exploration of the town itself as a preliminary wander, and that, combined with the return journey of two miles along the canal, will provide enjoyment enough for all.

From the car park head south-west, down the western bank of the canal along a narrow road. This passes an old manually-operated crane before heading along a private driveway. Signs point out that it is a no-through road, and that it is only open to walkers. The way passes to the right of a bungalow and soon emerges onto more open terrain with the infant River Hull to the right. Here you are entering the flatlands of the Hull Valley, hardly 30 feet above sea level. The inner curve of the main Wolds chain lies behind you, with the Capital of the Wolds nestling at its foot in an open hollow of good quality arable land.

Just beyond the bungalow, where we can also see the remains of the first lock on the canal, a bend to the left brings us around to an easterly heading. There were four locks on the main canal before it joined the Frodingham Beck and the River Hull, with a further lock at Hempholme to the north of Beverley. There was a further lock on the Beverley Beck and one on the Leven Canal, both at the point where they adjoined the main River Hull. Most of these can still be seen today, although our walk will take in only the first two.

The route onwards is obvious, following, as it does, the banks of the canal throughout. To the south the River Hull meanders a slow-moving course at close range, often passing within feet of the canal banks before turning away again on another tortuous bend.

It always amazes me how the river has cut such a devious course in what is apparently flat land. The clay bed would have been worn down gradually by the melt-water from the last ice age, taking thousands of years to find the course of least resistance through the carr lands at the river's head, whilst all the time succumbing to gravity's pull on its way to the tidal waters down the valley. But to talk of a valley here seems ludicrous. Chesney Farm, just across the canal to the north as you walk along, is a mere 11 metres above sea level, while the village of Wawne, just to the north of Hull, is only five metres above. Hardly any perceptible gradient at all – just seven metres drop in height over a distance of 11½ miles as the crow flies – a distance that can be doubled if you take into account every twist and turn of the river. Of course, if the River Hull were straighter it would lose some of its essential character. As it is, it fills the walker strolling along its banks with the desire to linger, to admire the views and the wildlife, and that is what these short outings into the countryside of the Wolds is all about.

Our way continues gently along the canal bank, eventually coming to another lock at a small bridge which leads over to the main road. You can walk along this road for just under a mile to Wansford for some liquid refreshment, if you feel the need, being aware of the traffic, though the delights of Great Driffield will probably be a greater attraction, in which case you should retrace your steps to the town.

Chapter Twenty Five

Bishop Wilton

Just to the south of Garrowby Hill, the steep gradient on the old Roman road now taken by the traffic heading east to the coast on the busy A166, a fresh water spring rises at the head of a deep wooded dale. The spring has carved the dale from the soft chalk of this western scarp of the Wolds, forming what is known locally as Worsen Dale. A minor road leaves the A166 just to the east of the summit of Garrowby Hill and takes infrequent traffic down and along the bed of the dale to the edges of the village of Bishop Wilton, one of the most picturesque villages in the whole of East Yorkshire. Our walk starts here.

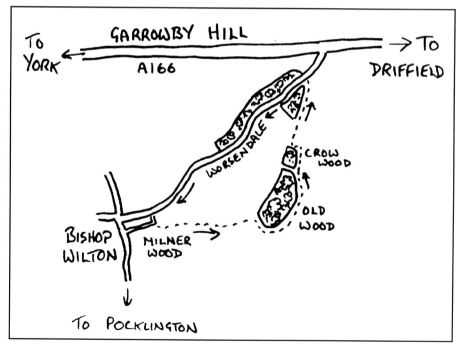

But first let's take a look at the village and its environs. St. Edith's Church throws up a glorious spire into the open skies above the village, and villagers still thank Sir Tatton Sykes, the 5th baronet, for his work in restoring their place of worship. He met the cost of hiring the architect J. L Pearson to undertake the work on this wonderful Norman church.

The village itself stands upon the site of a palace which the archbishops once had here, hence the name, though now the centre of village life is undoubtedly the well-known Fleece Hotel. This has welcomed and revived many a tired walker in its time, be they ramblers out for a short day trip on the Wolds, or long-distance walkers attempting either the 50-mile Minster Way or the 40-mile circular Chalkland Way, both of which pass through the village.

For walkers from further afield, the village has the distinction of giving its name to the highest hill in the whole of the county – Bishop Wilton Beacon. This is, however, a somewhat dubious distinction, as the A166 passes within a few feet of the 'summit' at 807 feet above sea level. Why such a humble eminence is recognised throughout the country is down to an ever-growing, fanatical band of 'list-tickers'. Hillwalkers in Scotland often start out for a day above the glens with the life-time ambition of climbing all of the mountains in that country above 3,000 feet high. These mountains are universally known as 'The Munros' after the man who

The pleasant little village of Bishop Wilton.

first compiled the full list. Likewise walkers heading for the hills of the Lake District tick off each hill they have done there, known collectively as 'The Wainwrights'. So, where does lowly Bishop Wilton Beacon fit into this strange scheme of things? In 1992 Alan Dawson drew up a list of all the hills in the British Isles, regardless of height, which have a drop of at least 150 metres on all sides before the next hill. This list was named 'The Marilyns', and Bishop Wilton Wold qualifies as one such hill, and indeed, as the only one in this Riding. In all there are a staggering 2,004 Marilyns throughout the length and breadth of the country, and nobody so far has climbed them all, although one or two people are close to it. I wonder what they'll make of Bishop Wilton Wold when they come to pull on their boots to 'tick' this Marilyn. Not only does the main road pass very close by the summit, thereby making any effort to 'climb' it seem rather silly, but the very top, an Ordnance Survey triangulation pillar [used for the original surveys, though now made obsolete by satellite surveys], stands within the grounds of a Yorkshire Water Authority property, replete with ample 'keep out' signs.

Close by the summit, the site of the old beacon is passed by the traffic to the south of the main road. This was a very important aid to communication within the nearby villages in its day, and it is known that it was made ready for lighting in 1588 as a precaution against a seemingly imminent invasion by the Spanish Armada. It was again prepared by local militia men during the Napoleonic Wars at the turn of the 19th century, but again it cannot be determined for certain whether or not the beacon was actually lit. By 1850 the tower had seen the last of its days and had disappeared from the East Riding landscape.

After a wander around the village, you will no doubt feel like coming to grips with the wonderful chalky hills which rise from within its boundary and dominate its skyline to the east. Narrow lanes follow both sides of the

beck, but ours is the one along its southern side. Near Mill House a public footpath sign points across the stream and into the scrubby pasture of Milner Wood. The beck itself flows on south-westwards, beyond the villages of Spittal near Fangfoss, Wilberfoss and Newton upon Derwent to join the oft-flooded plain of Thornton Ings beside the Pocklington Canal, although here at its source it is little more than a murmuring brook.

Our modest objective for the day is a round of the head of Worsendale, pronounced 'Wossndill' by the older residents of the village, and the way leads up the spit of land above the scrub of Hagworm Wood.

Higher up the slope, the bigger tree specimens of beech, ash and horse chestnut dot the hillside around the Old Wood. These chestnuts must surely provide the children of Bishop Wilton with a goodly supply of prize-winning conkers in autumn, so noble and stately do they rise above the dale.

The way soon levels out as a fence borders the upper limits of the Old Wood and the path begins to contour around above its boundaries. Gaps through the old tree cover reveal the distant, hazy smudges of the Pennines across the open plain of the Vale of York to the west, and on really clear days you can pick out the gritstone mountains of the Yorkshire Dales National Park across this flatness. These peaty whalebacks are old friends of mine, though it takes an intimate knowledge of those wonderful hills to be able to identify individual personalities among their ranked purple throngs from such a distance as this. Rarely does such a wide vista unfold so for me to recognise Buckden Pike or Great Whernside from this western scarp of the Wolds.

The public footpath continues gently around the flank of Worsendale, keeping close by the Old Wood throughout, until a line can be taken across a short field to the top end of Crow Wood, a more modern plantation of coniferous trees. From this point a public footpath branches off to the east and can be followed out to the minor lane that is the Beacon Road. Turning north along this brings you close by the original site of the beacon, in the field to the left just before reaching the main A166 York to Driffield road.

However, there is little to see there these days, and to reach the summit of Bishop Wilton Wold from here involves a lengthy plod along the very busy highway to the east and cannot be recommended.

Few readers of this book will want to take this detour to the site of the beacon, and so you should continue around Crow Wood, taking a brief downhill leg at a corner of the plantation. The way soon resumes its contouring predilection, before a steady climb begins to reach the very head of Worsendale to the north. Here we meet the minor road which comes down from the top of Garrowby Hill, and our way enjoys the benefits of this quiet country lane back to the village.

At first you will find yourself enclosed in a delightful wood where finches and titmice (the various members of the tit family of birds, such as blue tit, great tit etc.) hang from branches and flock gaily across the road, but soon the woods give way to the open pasture of Worsen Dale, where yellowhammers sing from hedge tops and sheep skip along the grassy slopes. The lane leads back to the village in a little less than a mile, where the weary will be glad to slake their thirst in the Fleece Hotel.

This is a walk to savour, and on such an outing picnics are always a good idea. In all, the walk is not much more than two miles in length, and, though the sensible will spend a good couple of hours doing the round of the dale, that amount of time is by no means necessary.

Appendix

Useful Addresses

Yorkshire Wildlife Trust
10 Toft Green
York
YO1 6JT
Telephone: 01904 659570

Hull Valley Wildlife Group
Membership Secretary
Jimmy James
238 Sigston Road
Beverley
East Yorkshire
HU17 9PL

Mr. R. Watson
(North Wolds Walk)
33 Sutherland Avenue
Hull
HU6 7UG

Dennis Parker
(High Hunsley Circuit)
11 Elmsall Drive
Beverley
East Yorkshire
HU17 7HL

Glen Hood
(Beverley 20)
329 Kingston Road
Willerby
HU10 6PY

Yorkshire Wolds Heritage Trust
Mr. M. Stanley
c/o Monument Buildings
Ferens Art Gallery
Queen Victoria Square
Hull
Tel: (01482) 613902

Yorkshire Wolds Buildings Preservation Trust
Dr. David Neave
29 Wood Lane
Beverley
HU17 8BS
Tel: (01482) 860310

The author can be contacted with regard to organised hillwalking and navigation courses on the following number: 01482 877472.